(EXTRA)ORDINARY

35 Men and Women of the Bible Whose Faith Changed Everything

M. D. CRACKOWER

WISE OWLS
PUBLISHING HOUSE

(EXTRA)ORDINARY

35 Men And Women of the Bible
Whose Faith Changed Everything

M. D. Crackower

Published by:
Wise Owls Publishing House

To contact the author: mdcrackower.com

ISBN: 979-8-9944057-0-3 (paperback)

(EXTRA)ORDINARY

35 Men and Women of the Bible
Whose Faith Changed Everything

DEDICATION

To those who stand in the shadows and keep the good fight,
Who will never stand on a stage or under the spotlights,
The Lord knows your deeds,
And your faith He sees.
You are not forgotten,
Neither are you forsaken.
You are part of something bigger
Than all of us together.

M.D. Crackower

"But those who wait on the Lord
Shall renew their strength;
They shall mount up with wings like eagles,
They shall run and not be weary,
They shall walk and not faint."
Isaiah 40:31

CONTENTS

LIST OF ILLUSTRATIONS

A FAITH HALL OF FAME FOR THE UNKNOWN

Dear Reader,

It all began twenty-two years ago, as I was discussing my latest read with a colleague during recess. I had just finished *The Viscount of Bragelonne* by Alexandre Dumas, the third massive 2,700-page volume of the beloved classic *The Three Musketeers*. This read was so fascinating that that's all I wanted to talk about. My colleague's reaction, however, left me speechless, but in a good way. This nearly retired elementary school teacher, who had spent his life in the classroom, was also an avid reader, perhaps more so than I; his words changed everything. They were simple, but what an impact they had. He said the magical words every reader wants to hear: "You made me want to read that book!" As soon as he pronounced these words, the Holy Spirit spoke to me: "This is what should happen when you talk about the Bible." As

I write the introduction to my second book today, twenty-two years later, I reminisce about these words that have never left my mind. If I can bring a man to want to read a 2,700-page work of fiction, what should it be when I talk about the only book that will bring freedom, life, and peace to the world? I became convinced that if I could get people to dig into the Bible, then the Holy Spirit would do the rest. If I could instill in people the desire to discover the wonderfully poetic and truthful texts and testimonies of the Old and New Testaments, lives would be transformed. I am a reader. Brick-type books don't scare me, but I understand what the perspective of opening a massive old book could be for others. So, I hope that by bringing these bite-sized testimonies, these specks of light drawn from the Bible, it will attract you toward the light. I hope you will discover and be encouraged by the wonderful truths of the Bible, its historical accuracy, and its uniqueness, and that you will want to delve, research, and learn more about the book that brings life. I hope you will be inspired to live a life that makes a difference, so that, as you share your love for the Word of God, you will hear these wonderful words too: "You made me want to read that book."

We all love a good story with a hero who wins against all odds at the end and overcomes every difficulty he encountered on his path. They inspire us. C. S. Lewis wrote in "On Three Ways of Writing for Children":

There is something ludicrous in the idea of so educating a generation that is born to the OGPU[1] and the atomic bomb. Since it is so likely that they will meet cruel enemies, let them at least have heard of brave knights and heroic courage. Otherwise you are making their destiny not brighter but darker... Let there be wicked kings and beheadings, battles and dungeons, giants and dragons, and let villains be soundly killed at the end of the book. Nothing will persuade me that this causes an ordinary child any kind or degree of fear beyond what it wants and needs to feel[2].

If fictional characters can have such a positive impact on children and their rearing, how much more can the true testimonies of the real men and women of the Bible? The Bible gives us examples of ordinary men and women who did extraordinary things in the face of evil, turning their world upside down. If I mentioned the name of King David, you would probably know who I am talking about, what he did, and what he was known for. The same goes for Moses, Elijah, Gideon, Paul, and Peter. Maybe you could even specify exactly where to find their stories or testimonies in the Bible. These are the great men of God, the great generals. Those who moved mountains, parted seas, and called fire down to earth. They led battles and won, they killed

---

1 The OGPU was the USSR's secret police and intelligence agency between 1923 and 1934. I preceded the better-known KGB and aimed at suppressing dissidents and counter-revolutionaries opposed to the Communist regime then in place. It was in charge, among other things, of the Gulag system and religious persecutions.
2 C. S. Lewis, *Of Other Worlds: Essays and Stories*, 31.

giants, and they held the rain for three years. They "conquered kingdoms, performed acts of righteousness, obtained promises, shut the mouths of lions, quenched the power of fire, escaped the edge of the sword, from weakness were made strong, became mighty in war, put foreign armies to flight" (Hebrews 11:33–34). To paraphrase Acts 17:6, they turned the world upside down. We understand their great works and why their names still resound so strongly in our ears. They are the fabric of movies that still amaze us.

However, more often than not, these great men and women of the Bible did not achieve victory alone. The Lord is not the Lord of the Great Isolated Generals, but the Lord of Hosts[3]. He is the Commander in Chief of an army made of men and women who worked and walked in the light and the shadows. Some are well-known, some are less so, and others remain anonymous. One day, He will reward everyone according to their deeds.

Ever since the Fall of man, the world has been the battlefield of a war raging between two very organized armies: Satan and his legions of demons on one side, the Lord and His heavenly hosts on the other. In between, humans are engaged, willingly picking a side: They are either for God or for Satan. There is no in-between in this war, which has a lot at stake. Every one of us must pick a side that will determine our eternal destination. Everyone is involved; everyone is concerned. Even if we already

––––––––––––––––

3   One of the names of the Lord most often mentioned in the Bible is the Lord of Hosts. This name appears 261 times in the Old Testament alone. "Host" is an Old English term that designates an army.

know the outcome of this war, God chose to fight this battle alongside us, and He gave us the power to change the eternity of our fellow humans through the Good News of Jesus Christ. The Lord will promote, use, and place in key posts those who prove themselves to be obedient, faithful, trustworthy, humble, and who walk in faith.

Hebrews states, "Now faith is the substance of things hoped for, the evidence of things not seen. For by it, the elders obtained a good testimony" (Hebrews 11:1 and 2). Everything came from faith. It was the root of all the greatest and smallest accomplishments that turned the world upside down. This book aims to continue what the author of the epistle to the Hebrews could not finish for lack of time: to develop the Hall of Fame of the Unknowns by focusing on these lesser-known soldiers who stood the test of time through their deeds and glorified the Lord. Most are everyday people, soldiers who never stood on a stage or led crowds. However, anonymity and obscurity were not an excuse for them to remain in the background and watch. They refused to dwell in mediocrity or rely on past glories. Paul wrote to Timothy that we don't have a spirit of shyness, but of power, wisdom, and love (2 Timothy 1:7). We can all wear these traits like a garment. The qualities Jesus possessed will empower us to stand and work for the Lord without seeking the glories of this world, and to walk in the shadows, for we are not made for this world. We walk, knowing that, even if pastors and leaders see neither us nor our work, we know and glorify in our anonymity because we build a kingdom that is not ours, a kingdom bigger than us. We know the Lord sees us and records all our deeds. His glory animates and motivates the soldiers who fight for something greater.

What more shall I say, for I want to tell of Shiphrah and Puah, Miriam, Barzillai, Ananias, Joseph of Arimathea, the people of Jabez-Gilead, Abigail, and Bezalel, who by faith stood against empires, defied emperors, saved the prophets, sought righteousness over comfort, and took God's side. Many worked in the shadows. Sometimes they are anonymous; sometimes they are known. Still, they changed the world. They were part of the Lord's army, His Stratos. They were soldiers, but they were more than that. It's by faith that they touched the Lord's heart with their prayers and their tears. It's by faith that they remained faithful unto death when everything was over or looked like it was. It's by faith that they walked with God and were taken. It's by faith that they did not fear men, knowing that the one with them was greater than the one standing against them. It's by faith that they put their talents in the service of the Lord, despising man's gold, preferring to delight in God's glory and His Kingdom. It's by faith that they never doubted. They were courageous and wise; they defied empires, choosing to fear the Lord over their warlord. It's their faith that impressed Jesus. In the end, it is by faith that all of them will hear, "Well done, good and faithful servant; you were faithful over a few things, I will make you ruler over many things. Enter into the joy of your lord" (Matthew 25:21).

Yes, we know the names of David, Gideon, and Moses, and we need men and women such as these. We understand their great works and why their names still resound so strongly in our ears.

However, just as no general is anything without an army behind him, those men would be nothing alone. David had thirty-seven valiant men who remained faithful to the end. Moses trained Joshua; Gideon had a father who stood alone against an angry religious crowd.

Above all, this book asks the question of what is truly important: Is it the idea that other people might see you? Or the fact that God knows you? We are not all destined to shine in the light of glory; we may be ordinary, and that's okay because we all have a mission to accomplish. We are part of an army. We are soldiers; we are God's *Stratos*.

As I close this letter, I want to thank you for picking up a copy of *(Extra)Ordinary*. I hope the lives of these thirty-five men and women will not only encourage you in your walk with Jesus but will also show you how you can make a difference (a big difference) where you are today, among your people, by making simple, sometimes easy, other times difficult, decisions. These are the heroes who fought for what is right and changed the world. May they encourage you to do the same, because with God, everything is possible.

There is no right or wrong way to read this book. You can either read it as a devotional, one person a day, over the course of a week, or you can read it through and let each one of these lives tell you their story and inspire you. Each chapter begins with the reading of the biblical text. So, if you do not own a Bible, make haste to find one. Alternatively, if you are hesitant about purchasing a Bible, there are excellent websites, such as

Biblegateway.com (https://www.biblegateway.com), that will allow you to read the texts for free.

Each person covered in this book follows the same development. Initially, I analyze how and why they were in the shadows, the circumstances that surrounded their lives, and the culture in which they lived, among other factors. Next, I describe how each person's actions and decisions changed everything. Lastly, all these men and women of the Bible are here to teach us and inspire us to make a difference. We can draw lessons from their examples.

To write this book, I used the Bible to explain the Bible and extracted the life principles that we can apply, teach, and use to make a difference in our lives and those around us. As an academic by training and trade, I researched the backgrounds of each and the historical contexts in which these ordinary men and women lived, highlighting how their decisions changed the world, went against the flow, and ultimately prevailed against all odds.

Lastly, I aimed to create a book that is both practical and useful for your daily life. At the end of each reading, I have added a set of questions to help you reflect on what you have read and how you can apply these principles in your daily life today. You can keep a journal where you write down your reflections and actions you can take to change your circumstances and the lives of those around you.

As you embark on this journey, let the heroes transport you and open your imagination to the possibilities that dwell in God.

To expand on C. S. Lewis' initial quote, let's watch them stand against wicked kings and win, fight battles and overcome, save entire cities without a fight, just because of wisdom. Learn from those who overcame and equip yourself to make the transition from ordinary to extraordinary so that, in the end, you will hear the Lord say to you, "Well done, good and faithful servant; you have been faithful over a few things, I will make you ruler over many things. Enter into the joy of your Lord" (Matthew 25:23).

Blessings in Christ,
M. D. Crackower

PART 1

Those Who Touched God's Heart

Illustration 1: Zacchaeus

The Bible states that God is a good Father, a perfect example who cares for His children. As a Father, He values obedience, respect, and devotion to Him. From the smallest to the greatest, we are all equal in His eyes, and we are offered the same plan of salvation through Jesus Christ. What we do with it, however, is our choice, and this Father's attention depends on our decision.

In the Bible, when one of the Lord's children cried out for mercy, His response was always timely, faith-building, and transformative. At least, that's what Hagar, Hannah, and Zacchaeus experienced. So, let's listen to their stories and see how they touched God's heart because that changed everything…

HAGAR

Mistreated, humiliated, cast away… If we were to list all the adjectives describing Hagar, they would portray a terrible life and a less-than-ideal position, even though she belonged to Abram's household. Yet, in her trials, she touched God's heart, and He blessed her by making her the mother of a nation: the Ishmaelites. Her story teaches us that no situation is too hopeless for the Lord to handle, nor are circumstances too desperate for Him to turn into blessings. So, let's begin by reviewing Hagar's circumstances and how she stood out through faith and obedience.

Hagar was a young Egyptian girl at the service of Sarai, Abram's wife. As such, she was exiled, deported, away from her people, her country, her culture, and her family. Maybe she was sold by her people as an enslaved person; perhaps she was an orphan!

They probably acquired her during their first stay in Egypt (Genesis 12:10–20), and she followed Abram and Sarai during their journeys. She remained faithfully at their service for almost ten years until that fateful day when Sarai gave her to Abram to beget a son.

Socially, Hagar was enslaved, with barely anything to her name except Ishmael, her son, whom she had with Abram. During her service, she fought for her survival multiple times. The author of Genesis tells us that Sarai had the right of life and death over Hagar. A right Sarai exercised two times out of jealousy. The first time Hagar found herself in a life-threatening situation was because of Sarai's anger. She tried to escape. However, the angel of the Lord saw her and asked that she return and serve Sarai and Abram, which she did (Genesis 16:9). The second time, her mistress's jealousy led her to be cast out from the safety of the group with her son. She was then sent to the desert with bread and a skin of water, not much to survive. She was condemned to die from thirst and hunger, and, on top of this, forced to witness her son die a slow and painful death. Despite these experiences, she was familiar with the Lord because she had lived under Abram's tent, and she had witnessed the meaning of true faith. Both times, the angel of the Lord appeared to her and saved her, and she obeyed His voice. Because of her obedience, she received the promise that she would beget a great nation through the son she had with Abram. Amid this terrible situation, the Lord made her a promise: He would save her and her son and make her descendants a great nation, on one condition: that she would keep obeying Him. "Return to your mistress, and submit yourself under her hand. (…) I will multiply your descendants exceedingly, so that they shall not be counted for multitude" (Genesis 16:10).

The story of Hagar and Ishmael comes right after the Lord promised to give Abram a posterity. Seeing nothing happening, Sarai, who probably knew of the promise, decided to take things into her own hands and forced her husband and her servant into a transaction that could potentially resolve her infertility problems. She wanted to create her miracle by forcing the hand of the Lord and bear her posterity through a substitutionary solution. This event is not the first of its kind. She notoriously did not trust the Lord: Remember that when the angel of the Lord met Abram at Mamre and announced that he would beget a son, she laughed. As her name indicates, she was bitter. This bitterness caused her to harbor resentment and anger, which blinded her to the power of the Lord. Unlike Hagar, she did not trust the Lord, despite seeing Abram, a man who walked in faith.

Hagar and Sarai's testimonies teach many universal, valuable lessons that can help each one of us today in our walk.

The first one is that seeing and believing are not enough. Living is essential. Sarai knew of the Lord, but she never trusted Him like Abram or Hagar. She laughed, she scolded, she berated, and she nagged. Do not rely only on what your eyes see, but walk in faith, trust the Lord, and live each day with His Kingdom in mind. The faith of the children delights the Lord because they show trust and confidence when they believe.

The second one is simple: Do not try to create your own miracle through human means like Sarai did. Human solutions are often tainted with sin and constitute temporary fixes that will not last. They will eventually crumble under your feet, betray you, or turn against you. God's timing is His greatest miracle. He is never late, nor is He early.

The third is a promise that comes straight from the Bible: Jesus said that the eyes of the Lord are on the sparrow (Matthew 6:25–27), and that not one hair falls from your head that He doesn't know about (Luke 21:18). Your eyes (and mine) limit our understanding of the true nature of power from above because we rely on nature, rather than on the spiritual. If this is you (I know I was like this), lift your eyes to the Lord, and know that He is with you. Keep His Law and commands in your heart, feed your soul with them, and stay away from sin. Spiritual forces surround us and are at work 24/7. "Behold, He who keeps Israel shall neither slumber nor sleep" (Psalms 121:4).

In conclusion, the Lord hears the voices of those who are lost, exiled, distant, or suffering. In His love, He desires to bless them. However, there are conditions: We must return to Him, stay faithful, and obey His commands. When away from the Lord, we try to find a way out by earthly means, as Sarai did. We even attempt to create our own miracle. However, this only delays the hand of the Lord, causes troubles, or could potentially cancel His blessings. Those who are far must draw closer to the Lord and bridge the cultural gaps that the world fosters through its ideologies and philosophies. Those who are exiled must find their way back to the presence of the Lord. Suffering can silence the voice of the Lord or make it more difficult to hear, as suffering draws all attention. So, wait on the Lord. Your tears will not go unnoticed. When He draws nearer, be ready to follow and obey Him. All that remains after that is to watch His hand perform the miracle. Refresh your mind with scriptures. Write down the promises you received, the dreams you had, and go over them often. His promises are for you if you choose to rely on and trust Him.

WALK BY FAITH EVERY DAY

"But those who wait on the Lord
Shall renew their strength.
They shall mount up with wings like eagles,
They shall run and not be weary,
They shall walk and not faint" (Isaiah 40:31)

REFLECTION QUESTIONS

Consider the path Hagar followed, everything she went through, and the blessings she received in the end. How can the lives and the testimonies of the men and women of the Bible encourage you to keep on walking and grow in your knowledge of the Lord?

Which one of Hagar's life lessons inspired you the most in today's reading?

HANNAH

Reading: 1 Samuel 1 and 2

As soldiers in the army of the Lord, we have access to the Great General, the Great Provider, the Almighty. Unlike what some religions or beliefs claim, He is not withdrawn from His Creation; instead, He desires to be involved. His involvement in our lives is conditioned by our willingness to let Him in and our prayers. Our desperate, faithful prayers can not only touch His heart but also move His arm. More importantly, these prayers, even the silent ones, have the power to change history.

Hannah is here to teach us this lesson. So, who was Hannah, and how did she make a difference?

Hannah was one of the wives of a man named Elkanah from the tribe of Ephraim. Elkanah was a very devout man who loved his wife and favored her over his second wife, Peninnah.

However, Hannah seemed not to have God's favor because she was barren, and Peninnah, mother to multiple children, stood as a conquering rival to her. It appears that, in addition, Peninnah took a particular pleasure in reminding Hannah of her inability to have children. In those days, being barren was a heavy stigma, almost like a curse.

Every year, Elkanah and his family went to Shiloh to sacrifice to the Lord. And every year, Hannah dreaded this moment because Peninnah constantly reminded her of her failure through nagging. There was nothing Hannah could do to stop Peninnah from nagging at her. Not even Elkanah's kindness and favor were enough to provide her with some relief. Translated into modern language, her situation says that despite living in a family that belonged to the Lord, she had no power to change her situation by herself.

She stood every day in the presence of the Lord through her husband because of his devotion and faithfulness, which extended over the family and guided their life and routine. In modern terms, Hannah had a church. She also faced the presence of failure because she was childless, and there was nothing Elkanah could do to fix it. Despite being part of a devoted family, she could not overcome the daily struggle. Being part of that family was not enough. In modern terms, the church was not enough. However, if we compare Hannah to other women of the Bible who experienced the same thing, namely Sarai and Rachel, Hannah's reaction differs. Sarai became bitter and ironic about her state and age, laughing at the news of her coming pregnancy. Rachel nagged at her husband, constantly provoking his anger: "Am I God?" he said. Hannah never rebuked the Lord or asked why nature made her that way. One year, brokenhearted, Hannah decided that something had to be done, and that only the Lord could do it. She decided to go alone to the power source of everything, located within the Tabernacle, God Himself, to cry her heart out. She entered the presence of the Lord and stopped relying on others' faith and traditions. It was a one-on-one conversation, a direct plea.

Still, even in the House of the Lord, someone stood between her and the Lord: Eli, the high priest who had allowed corruption and perversion to enter the walls of the House of God. Eli impersonated religion. Cold, judgmental, away from the truth, religion. And religion broke Hannah's heart. As she walked silently in prayer, her lips alone moving, Eli, in his prominent priest garment, status, apparat, and function, called her a drunkard! He looked at appearances and ignored her true motives and suffering.

I can only imagine how Hannah felt as she desperately called the Lord for help and was called a drunkard. I can only imagine what happened in the Lord's heart when He heard His daughter's cries and desperation, and witnessed Eli's religious reaction so contrary to His nature. Hannah had just made a vow to the Lord to devote her firstborn son to Him if He granted her the desires of her heart. However, despite the potential for offense and self-righteousness to take root in her heart due to Eli's reaction, Hannah persevered. She boldly expressed her heart's desires and desperation out loud: "I was pouring out my soul to the Lord…I have been praying here out of great anguish and grief," she said (1 Samuel 1:16). Her prayers, devoid of religious pretense, touched God's heart.

Hannah prayed in the shadows, pleading her cause to the Lord, and she touched His heart. Her prayer changed the spiritual landscape of Israel. She had a son whom she named Samuel. Now, think about who Samuel was for a minute: He was a prophet, the last judge in Israel, and King Saul and David's advisor. He was the one the Lord woke up at night to talk to, the one who restored righteousness and justice in the House of the Lord and to the people in worship. We would not have had a Samuel or a David if it were not for Hannah's fervent, desperate prayer and faith.

When Eli realized his error, he stood back and blessed her. Then she left. What happens next is fascinating: Verse 18 says that Hannah went her way, "and ate something and her face was no longer downcast" (v. 18). She left differently than she came in. Before, she was refusing to eat. Afterward, she was eating. Before, she was sad and grieving. Afterward, her face was different.

Her situation had not changed. She was not pregnant. She had not even received the certainty that she would. But she knew one thing she didn't know before: She had stood in the presence of the Lord and made her request heard. That changed the way she perceived things. Whatever came next, she was ready for it. Entering the presence of the Lord by bypassing religion and traditions transformed her in her whole being, whatever the result. Then, true worship followed, which she did the next day (1 Samuel 2:19). Now, she knew Him, and later wrote the beautiful psalm of chapter 2, found in 1 Samuel. True worship, as demonstrated by Hannah, is not just about singing hymns or attending church services. It is about living a life that is pleasing to God, in gratitude for His faithfulness and the answers to our prayers. However, the story of Hannah does not stop there. Verse 19 states that Elkanah knew his wife, and that she became pregnant within that same year. She had a son, whom she named Samuel.

Many Christians today find themselves in a difficult situation, much like Hannah. They know of a power that is within reach, but they fail to fix what is broken in their life because instead of calling upon this power, they struggle to fix things on their own, or they rely on someone else's faith, a routine of going to church, or hanging out with people of faith. What is missing? A personal engagement to go to the source of power in person and not to rely on the flow of events, religiosity, or belonging to a particular group. They follow the belief that we are enough to fix our problems. But sin is stronger.

There is great power within reach for those who believe and trust in the Lord and live according to His Laws. However, the average person struggles with sin even within the church because they do not go to the source of that power or know it personally. Every Sunday, they are torn between truth and blinding, nagging Peninnah-type lies. To Hannah, this was a constant state (1 Samuel 1:17): "Every time…Every year." There was no way out of it.

Peter writes in 1 Peter 5:7: "Therefore humble yourselves under the mighty hand of God that He may exalt you in due time, casting all your care upon Him, for He cares for you." Why resist doing what Hannah did? Bring your struggles, desires, and fears to the feet of Jesus and leave them there. Please don't pick them back up by constantly thinking about them. That's Peninnah's nagging. You are your own Peninnah sometimes, reminding yourself continually how inadequate you are because you lose sight of the Lord and focus on circumstances instead. Once you cast them down at the feet of Jesus, they must stay there. You shouldn't think about them, talk about them, and sometimes you should give them up to Christ and stop praying about them. Like Hannah, go to the Lord, then eat and change your face. This is trust in action!

Prayers—silent, desperate intercessory, or conversational—can change the course of history. You might never see their results or accomplishments in your time. I don't know if Hannah saw Samuel become a prophet, crown David king, judge Israel, or choose Saul. Not only did these things happen, but they also mattered. Samuel was who he was partly because of his mother. Your prayers leave a mark on the future. They are a legacy made to future generations. They stand before the Lord like perfume constantly going up.

Hannah's story ends in chapter 2 with a psalm she wrote. Her worship was different because it was true. Her faith became solid because, instead of relying on religion, circumstances, and traditions, she looked up to the source of power, rather than listening to a nagging voice that kept her down. Remember that this voice came from inside the family; she decided to rely on the Lord Himself and established a genuine relationship with God. Later, she went on to have more children: three sons and two daughters.

Hannah was a soldier in the Lord's army. His *Stratos*. A soldier of the shadows who touched God's heart and changed history for good. We won't all stand in the spotlight, but who knows what the Lord can do with one simple, genuine prayer? And that is what is most important…

WALK BY FAITH EVERY DAY

"Come to Me, all you who labor and are heavy laden, and I will give you rest. Take My yoke upon you and learn from Me, for I am gentle and lowly in heart, and you will find rest for your souls. For My yoke is easy, and My burden is light" (Matthew 11 28–30).

REFLECTION QUESTIONS

Hannah found herself in a difficult place: love on one side, and hate on the other. Even if her husband's love was true and strong, she kept on looking and being affected by Peninnah's nagging. Do you find yourself, or do you know someone, in this situation, sometimes focusing on the negative instead of the positive? What can you do today to change your perception (or theirs) of your (their) circumstances? What can you do today to show the Lord you will trust Him, whatever happens next?

ZACCHAEUS

Reading: Luke 19:1-10

Jesus famously told His disciples that "it is easier for a camel to go through the eye of a needle than for a rich man to enter the kingdom of God" (Luke 18:25). These well-known words followed an encounter with a wealthy young ruler who left Jesus sad because he did not want to part with his riches. In response, the confused followers asked, "Who can then be saved?" Jesus' reply was confident and hopeful: "The things which are impossible with men are possible with God" (Luke 18:27). The lesson could have ended there. However, Jesus, being the master teacher and God in the flesh, did not leave His words without application. This is evident in the teaching moment recorded in Luke 18, followed by the story of Zacchaeus in Luke 19, which serves as a real-life illustration of Jesus' words.

The name Zacchaeus means "pure" or "innocent" in Hebrew. Ironically, this name was in sharp contrast to its bearer's job and reputation as a tax collector. Zacchaeus was a Jew living in Jericho during Jesus' time. He was also a publican and the chief tax collector, a role that was highly disliked among the Jews, especially the Pharisees. Socially, he was regarded as being on the same level as a prostitute and a traitor.

This occupation, seen as a collaboration with the impure Romans, was also synonymous with corruption and greed, further fueling the societal disdain toward Zacchaeus. Tax collectors were known to ask more of the people than the actual tax rate. Corruption, theft, and extortion were part of his daily activities. In short, he was a sinner, he knew it, and he did not hide it. It was public knowledge!

As Jesus passed through Jericho on his way to Jerusalem, Zacchaeus, who had heard of him, desired to see the Son of Man. Jesus, knowing all thoughts, hearts, and motivations, found Zacchaeus hanging out in a tree. Following this initial encounter, Jesus entered the house of Zacchaeus. In a remarkable turn of events, after listening to Jesus' teachings, Zacchaeus, the despised, greedy, treacherous tax collector, repented of his sins and was transformed into a generous man, giving away his wealth to the poor and making right with those he had wronged. This stunning transformation serves as a demonstration that, although it is difficult for wealthy men to be saved, it is not impossible through God's grace and power. Zacchaeus' salvation illustrates that everything is possible with God, just like Jesus told His disciples one chapter earlier.

However, things did not happen on their own. Zacchaeus had to take steps to come to Jesus.

It all began with a burning desire to see Jesus. To reach his goal and catch a glance at Jesus, Zacchaeus had to overcome several obstacles. First, he was caught behind a wall. A crowd surrounded Jesus, making it impossible for him to come close or even see Jesus. So, by climbing a tree, Zacchaeus went above and beyond the average crowd member, demonstrating his unwavering determination and perseverance to get a glance of Jesus.

Second, when everybody joined a crowd, he went over it. Zacchaeus was of small stature and could not even count on biology to help him in his endeavor. He had to find a way to rise above the crowd, so he climbed a sycamore tree. We can make all kinds of excuses to stay away from Jesus, some of which are rooted in our very being: "That's just who I am! I can't help it," etc. Zacchaeus did not allow his circumstances to define him. He defied expectations and climbed a tree. This was a daring and unconventional move, but one that showed his determination to see Jesus despite all odds. However, the sycamore solution was temporary. Sycamore trees are easily noticeable due to their twisted trunks and are very susceptible to decay, making them hazardous for humans who attempt to climb their branches. This tree illustrates the fragile and twisted ways humans find solutions to their problems.

Once Jesus answered his silent call, Zacchaeus did not wait. Luke writes that he came down the tree with haste and joy. Then, once inside the house, as they were having dinner, Zacchaeus was transformed by listening to Jesus' teachings. He understood that he was a sinner in need of a Savior. He repented. The fruits of a changed life followed this repentance. He made generous donations to the people of Jericho, whom he had stolen from. He cut all ties with his old sins.

Zacchaeus' testimony highlights the potential for redemption for all sinners and the transformation of one's character, which is ultimately realized in his encounter with Jesus. His life was never the same again.

So how can Zacchaeus teach us today? First, do not be scared by the crowds who will block your access to Jesus. When Jesus comes near you, crowds will accumulate to prevent you from meeting him. Crowds represent people and their good intentions, but they can also symbolize the stresses of life, the worries, and the fears that cloud your vision and keep you at a distance from Jesus Christ. Go above, go around, go beyond, but do not let them keep you away from Jesus. When you need Him, go to Him by every means possible.

Second, attract Jesus' attention. The Gospels are full of examples of people who wanted to attract Jesus' attention and did everything in their power to see Him: screaming, touching His garment, calling, and destroying roofs. Climb a tree if you need to! Jesus will not despise those who genuinely want to meet Him and are searching for the truth. He will not remain insensitive to your desperate calling. God the Father promised that He would be with us every day and He would take care of us if we stayed in His presence and followed His Law. If you are not yet part of His people, then His passing through your life right now, your Jericho, is an opportunity to get saved and see your life take a complete turn away from sin. Do not waste this opportunity.

Third, do not delay; once you hear Jesus' call, respond quickly. Invite Jesus to enter and dwell in your house. Joy will fill your heart because you will understand the power of repentance and salvation, be freed from sin, and gain the strength to overcome it. You will never be alone again.

Fourth, your repentance will be evident, and you will bear fruit like Zacchaeus did. Indeed, he returned what he had stolen with interest and never sinned again. Did he become a disciple and follow Jesus around Galilee? No, he stayed in Jericho and became a walking reminder of God's transforming power. Zacchaeus became a living testimony and had to live by these new standards in the public eye. We know he lived a righteous life after that because if that were not the case, Luke would have never included his testimony in his writings.

In conclusion, Zacchaeus' testimony, found in Luke 19, comes after Luke 18, where Jesus shares the parable of the Publican and the Pharisee. In this parable, the publican repents from his sins, just like Zacchaeus did. Zacchaeus' story demonstrates that repentance and salvation are possible, even for those considered the worst sinners. In the second part of chapter 18, Jesus says that it is difficult for wealthy people to be saved, explaining that it would be easier for a camel to go through the eye of a needle. Yet, Jesus also states in the same chapter that what is impossible for men is possible with God. Zacchaeus was a wealthy man who found salvation and gave away a significant portion of his wealth. To Jesus' followers and the Pharisees, he demonstrated that sinners could repent, that rich men could be saved, and that God makes the impossible possible.

WALK BY FAITH EVERY DAY

"The Lord, the Lord God, merciful and gracious, longsuffering, and abounding in goodness and truth" (Exodus 34:6).

REFLECTION QUESTIONS

All odds were against Zacchaeus: society, biology, employment. However, they did not prevent Zacchaeus from searching for the Light of the World, Jesus.

Like Zacchaeus, how can you overcome all the odds standing against you today? What steps can you take to get Jesus' attention? What can you do to stop listening to the crowds trying to hold you back

PART 2

Those Who Remained Faithful

Illustration 2: Barzillai and King David

In the parable of the good servant found in Matthew 25:14–30, the master rewards the servant not for his diligence, his skillset, or his being busy, but for his faithfulness. The Lord values faithfulness and obedience above everything. Obed-Edom, Barzillai, and the people of Jabes-Gilead are here to teach us how to remain faithful in difficult times.

OBED-EDOM

When the Lord established His covenant with Israel at Mount Sinai (Exodus, Leviticus, and Deuteronomy), He made them the promises that if they followed His Laws and kept His commandments, He would bless them "for a thousand generations" (Deuteronomy 7:9). Later on, in same chapter, the nature of the blessings is described as "He (the Lord) will love you, and multiply you; He will also bless the fruit of your womb and the fruit of your land (…); there shall be not a male or female barren among you or your livestock" (Deuteronomy 7:14). Obed-Edom was the living testimony of the realization of the Lord's promises.

Obed-Edom ("Servant of Edom" in Hebrew) was a Levite who lived in the Gath region, on the border between Judah and Philistia, in a town called Kiriath Jearim. His house became the dwelling of the Ark of the Covenant, and he and his family served the Lord for months when everybody had abandoned Him. To fully understand the bearing of Obed-Edom's obedience and faithfulness, we must return to the fourth chapter of 1 Samuel, well before his time. In those days, Israel did not have a king; it was ruled by judges[4], and the Ark remained in Shiloh, within the Tabernacle. At the time this story begins, Eli combined the duties of the high priest in the Tabernacle and judge. However, Eli had allowed his sons, Hophni and Phineas, who were also priests of the Lord, to slip away from the truth and steal from the sacrifices made to the Lord. They also did things with the women who served at the entrance of the Tabernacle. Eli did nothing to stop them. This behavior contaminated the rest of Israel, who fell into sin, and, therefore, the Lord did not protect Israel from its enemies anymore. Israel was defeated by the Philistines (1067 BC), who took the Ark of the Covenant and brought it to Ashdod, their city, where they placed it in the temple of their god, Dagon. The Ark remained in Philistia for seven months. The Philistines experienced the wrath of God during these seven months and decided to get rid of the Ark. They placed it on a chariot pulled by cows and left it to its fate. The cows pulled the chariot to another city named Beth Shemesh, where it remained for an unspecified period (calculations indicate approximately forty years). Then, the Ark was moved to Kirjath-jearim, where it stayed in the house of Abinadab for twenty years. King Saul, then the ruler of Israel, did not bother with it.

---

4 Some example of these judges are: Gideon, Samson, Deborah, and Jephthah.

Eventually, in 1004 BC, King David decided to retrieve the Ark of the Covenant and bring it back to Jerusalem. Although his intentions were honorable, he did not follow the instructions given to Moses regarding its transportation: Uzzah died for trespassing on the Ark's rights, struck by the Lord. He had touched the Ark, which was absolutely forbidden (2 Samuel 6:7). Following these dramatic events, fear seized everyone, including King David, who changed his plans and abandoned the Ark of the Covenant in Gath, placing it in the house of Obed-Edom. David returned to Jerusalem angry and fearful.

The Ark remained in Obed-Edom's house for three months. Because he was a Levite, he was familiar with the rules and regulations that its care demanded. He also fully understood the extent and meaning of hosting such a holy object. The Lord dwelt in this house for three months, and Obed-Edom probably gave it all the respect it was due because, contrary to everyone before, the Bible shows that his home did not get cursed. It had to be something else to live in proximity to such a historical and sacred object! Curiosity probably showed its nose at the door. Greed and power grab probably knocked too. But in all things, Obed-Edom remained the servant and the keeper of the Ark. Consequently, "The Lord blessed Obed-Edom and all his household" (2 Samuel 6:11) just as He had promised in Deuteronomy 7:9.

I began this chapter with a verse from Deuteronomy 7, describing the blessings given to those who love and follow the Lord's commandments. The authors of 2 Samuel and 1 Chronicles explain that Obed-Edom was blessed in many ways exactly as described in the Mosaic Law in Deuteronomy 7. The promises made in Deuteronomy 7 speak about blessings in the form of children who are healthy and valiant. Obed-Edom was fruitful after the events mentioned in 2 Samuel 6. 1 Chronicles 26:8 states that Obed-Edom had eight sons, "because the Lord had blessed him." It is also mentioned that these sons were all valiant men who entered the service of the Lord, full of might and vigor. In His generosity, the Lord blessed the father of the family, and the blessings extended to his descendants. A total of sixty-two brave men came from Obed-Edom's family. Compared to the other gatekeepers of the temple, his family was the largest.

Second, his family received a promotion: Obed-Edom became the official keeper of the Ark and the guardian of the Mercy Seat after its return to Jerusalem. The Lord rewarded him and his sons for all their service by making them temple gatekeepers under King Solomon. They became trusted officials who protected the rooms and treasures in the House of the Lord. His children were found to be as trustworthy as their father.

Third, even after the Ark left his house, blessings continued to flow. 1 Chronicles tells us that the blessings did not leave with the Ark but persisted afterward. God's blessings are like a family legacy for "a thousand generations" (Deuteronomy 7:9). These blessings were not a secret. They were visible to all, and the echoes of them ran through Judah to the ears of David, who wanted his share of them. Recovered from his anger and terror, David came to Obed Edom's house after three months, this time disposed to follow God's directions and bring the Ark of the Covenant with him to Jerusalem.

There are three lessons from Obed-Edom's testimony that we can apply to our lives today. The first lesson is that Obed-Edom stood firm and remained faithful when everyone else left. David returned to his palace, his armies to Jerusalem, the people to their homes, all fearful and angered. Obed-Edom demonstrated loyalty to the Lord by accepting that the Ark remained under his roof. He was well-versed in the Law and the management of the sacred objects because he was a Levite, a member of the tribe devoted to the Tabernacle and the service of the Lord. Because of his faithfulness, God blessed him, and the blessings flowed over his family. Blessings are not meant to be kept by one person; instead, they flow in a cascade across future generations and extend to those living today.

The second lesson states that if you uphold the Laws of the Lord in your home and never compromise, everyone under your roof will be blessed. The Ark of the Covenant was a natural representation of the Lord's presence among humans, with the Mercy Seat as the place where the divine presence dwelt. Rejecting it was equivalent to rejecting the Lord.

The third lesson is that he did not fear death when it just happened because of the Ark. Obed-Edom was found faithful and respectful of the Lord's Laws and the Ark. Over time, his service and the blessings that ensued did not go unnoticed. It caught the ear of King David, who remembered the Ark left behind, and the eye of the Lord who saw a man faithful and trusting.

Faithfulness and loyalty created a legacy that impacted many, including the people of Israel, as Obed-Edom's sons served in the temple in the public eye. One simple act of obedience and faithfulness in service sparked countless blessings. That's a legacy worth leaving! Like Obed-Edom, choose to fear the Lord and revere His presence in your house. If you do so, you will benefit from His advice, His wisdom, which defies all human wisdom and knowledge, and blessings will flow from you to those who come after you, and around you. Don't compromise. If you even so slightly open your door to sin, it will enter like a wind, break everything. May your conduct be dictated by a conscience and ethics founded on the Word of God and the truth. Do not fear, for you will not be alone. Every day, the Holy Spirit will be there to give you the strength and the power to do what is right. You will be free not to sin. Your faithfulness in small things will teach you to be faithful in bigger things as well.

WALK BY FAITH EVERY DAY

"Therefore know that the Lord your God, He is God, the faithful God who keeps covenant and mercy for a thousand generations with those who love Him and keep His commandments; and He repays those who hate Him to their face, to destroy them. He will not be slack with him who hates Him; He will repay him to his face. Therefore you shall keep the commandment, the statutes, and the judgments which I command you today, to observe them" (Deuteronomy 7:9–11).

REFLECTION QUESTIONS

How did Eli, King Saul, King David, and Obed-Edom differ when they were near the Ark of the Covenant? Can your actions today bless those who will follow you and be around you? How?

BARZILLAI

What legacy will we leave to our children and our children's children? Deuteronomy 7:9 says that the Lord will bless those who love Him and keep His commandments for a thousand generations. Barzillai's goodness shone in God's eyes, and he was blessed among the Israelites, him and his descendants.

The name Barzillai means "made of iron" in Hebrew. Indeed, this man never deviated from the line of conduct that defined his behavior toward other human beings, hierarchy, and the Lord. His life was marked by generosity, loyalty, and goodness, following the Lord's commands. Barzillai lived under the reigns of Kings Saul and David. He was a wealthy man from the city of Rogelim, and a Gileadite, likely a descendant of the tribe of Manasseh. He lived in the northern region of modern Israel, specifically in the Gilead area.

The first time we hear about him, he is eighty years old.

When David faced his son Absalom's revolt, he escaped to the desert with his people. Absalom was determined to seize the throne through a *coup d'état* and was even willing to kill his father to reach his goals. Various people came to support the king during his forced exile. Barzillai and Shimei were some of them. Barzillai provided for the living and settling of David and all his people. The king left with his entire household: all his servants, all the Cherethites who lived in the palace, all the Pelethites and all the Gittites (six hundred men from Gath, the wives, and the children according to 2 Samuel 15:18). That makes over one thousand people fleeing with the king. He left ten concubines to keep the royal house.

After a while in the desert, David moved toward Menahaim, passing the Jordan River. There, he found refuge and resources through Barzillai, who cared for the king and all his people during their stay in Menahaim. Barzillai chose to remain faithful to the king, even when there was a risk of a *coup d'état*, knowing the potentially devastating consequences that would ensue if David abdicated to his son.

Barzillai was wealthy and highly regarded in his city. He had resources. Unlike many, he was not greedy; instead, he put his resources to serving the king. The Bible says that he and other men, Shobi, son of Nahash, Machir, son of Ammiel, brought: "beds and basins, earthen vessels and wheat, barley and flour, parched grain and beans, lentils and parched seeds, honey and curds, sheep and cheese of the herd, for David and the people who were with him to eat. For they said, 'The people are hungry and weary and thirsty in the wilderness'" (2 Samuel 17:28–29). They ensured there was enough food and supplies to feed the one thousand people. That accompanied King David. However, Barzillai did not consider the cost. He provided for everyone out of generosity and a spirit of service. He was so considerate that he prioritized the welfare of others and viewed his wealth to improve the lives of others.

When the king wanted to pay him back by inviting him to live at the court, he declined, but he asked King David to take care of his servant Chimham, which the king accepted. He detoured the blessings aimed at him for his servants. His servant was blessed from his goodness; he joined the king's court and was cared for the rest of his life. Also, the man's goodness benefited his descendants. David recommended only Barzillai's descendants to Solomon: "But show kindness to the sons of Barzillai the Gileadite, and let them be among those who eat at your table, for so they came to me when I fled from Absalom your brother" (2 Samuel). All the other people mentioned by the king in his final recommendations to Solomon were to be put to death.

May we understand that we are only vessels of the blessings given to us; let us use them wisely for the good and service of the Lord. What legacy shall we leave after us?

WALK BY FAITH EVERY DAY

"But that no one is justified by the law in the sight of God *is* evident, for "the just shall live by faith" (Galatians 3:11).

REFLECTION QUESTIONS

Consider what type of legacy you want to leave. What can you do today to change that legacy for the better?

What kind of difference did Barzillai make in the lives of King David and his people? What character traits does his actions reveal? How can you, like Barzillai, influence the lives of others today?

THE PEOPLE OF JABESH-GILEAD

Reading: 1 Samuel 31:8-13 and 2 Samuel 2:4-7

Making the right decision is hard when we are in defeat, left to our own devices, and no one is here to guide us. The people of Jabesh-Gilead found themselves without a king or leader after suffering a terrible defeat at the hands of the Philistines. Yet, they displayed remarkable courage, coming together and allowing their conscience to guide them in doing what was right in the eyes of the Lord, their fellow man, and in the face of their enemies. Their actions, a testament to their unwavering courage, played a key role in God's plan and brought them the wonderful reward of the new king's blessings.

In the time of King David, Jabesh-Gilead was a small town of little consequence located in the region of Gilead, east of the

Jordan River. It belonged to the half-tribe of Manasseh. In 1 Samuel 31, the inhabitants of Jabesh-Gilead made the decision not to fear the Philistines and to right a wrong. Israel had just suffered its most significant defeat against the Philistines on Mount Gilboa when King Saul and his three sons, including one who was to inherit the throne of Israel, tragically died, leaving the people without leadership and direction. Following the announcement of the death of the king and his sons, the Israelite soldiers forsook their cities. They fled away from the battlefield (1 Samuel 31:7). The next day, as if the death of Saul was not enough, the people of Israel woke up to hear of the terrible treatment the Philistines had inflicted on the king and his three sons' bodies (including Jonathan).

If the deeds of the Philistines exemplify Satan's strategy to deter us, the reaction of the inhabitants of Jabesh-Gilead teaches us what to do when facing such situations.

In 1 Samuel, we see two reactions to the same situation. On one side, we have the winners of the battle, the Philistines, a cruel pagan people known for their ruthless tactics and disregard for human life. On the other side, we have the losers, the Israelites who fled away, and were the losers at that point. However, the inhabitants of Jabesh-Gilead were also God-fearing Israelites. We read that the Philistines took the king's weapons and those of his sons as war prizes and beheaded them. After that, they spread the word among their fellow Philistines throughout their country and rejoiced. As if this were not enough, the Philistines exposed the beheaded bodies of the king and his sons on the walls of Beth-Shan for all to see, exposing them to the elements, the animals, national shame, and humiliation. This strategy was designed to deter their enemies, to instill fear, and discourage resistance or retaliation through visions of terror. It's a form of psychological warfare, a tactic the Philistines were known for.

As the Israelites had fled away to the mountains to hide, and they forsook their cities and belongings after the announcement of the king's death, the valiant men of Jabesh-Gilead stood up, went out of their city walls, and walked in the middle of the enemy camp to retrieve what they considered theirs: the body of their king and three sons. Yes, they had lost the battle; however, they did not consider themselves vanquished. Their actions were not just a display of courage but a testament to their faith in God's plan and loyalty to the king of Israel. Their mission became their sole focus, and they did not rest until the work was complete. They walked by night as soon as they heard the news, determined and focused, fueled by their faith in God's guidance and protection.

In this defeat, the Israelites suffered a significant loss: their king, leader, and heir to the throne. Things were very uncertain. However, we should be like the inhabitants of Jabesh, who did not allow defeat and uncertainty to discourage them from doing the right thing. Perhaps the Israelites lost; however, the men of Jabesh kept their heads up. Defeat is not permanent in life, not until we say so. Let's learn from our mistakes, find ways to make a difference, and still emerge as winners. Sometimes we win; sometimes we don't. It's not a reason to give up, because we will have plenty of other battles to turn wrongs into rights. We are on the Lord's side, and we know He will have the final word.

After all, following Saul's death, David became king of Israel, and he defeated the Philistines.

When facing defeat or danger, you can react in two ways: fight or flee. Yes, some things can scare you to death, push you into hiding, and lead you to turn your head the opposite way. But is that the solution? Your trials don't disappear because you turn your head away. Trials and problems will remain until you confront and address them. Just as the men of Jabesh walked all night to reach Beth-Shean, stay focused on your spiritual mission and calling. Do not let the distractions of the day or apparent defeats deter you from accomplishing the work of the Lord. Jesus sent us with one mission: to go around the world and make disciples. Spread the Good News, and never cease praying. Keep the goal in mind; keep the end in mind!

The Philistines' boastful actions exemplify Satan's character; he will delight in exposing your defeats to the public eye to humiliate you, ridicule you, discourage you, and scare you. To this end, he is willing to do anything, including exposing others' defeats to instill fear, thereby preventing you from acting and risking the enduring treatment. Satan uses psychological warfare as well as physical warfare. He will use every tool in his possession or at his reach to destroy you. However, remember that, as believers, you are not alone. You have at your disposal the armor of God to withstand these attacks. Satan will try to paralyze you by taking away your weapons, silencing your prayer life, confusing you to prevent you from thinking straight, and encouraging you to listen to the voices of fear and anxiety instead of lifting your eyes to the Lord. Satan will boast about what he did to you. He will discourage you from trying one more time, all to prevent you from reaching the breakthrough. Please do not listen to him. Quiet all the voices of doubt, anxiety, fear, anger, and resentment. Lift your eyes to the Lord, seek advice from like-minded individuals, and renew your strength like the eagle.

The story of the inhabitants of Jabesh-Gilead does not end in chapter 31. As these valiant men finished the work, they burnt the bodies and offered them a proper burial. Eventually, they received praise and blessing from King David for doing what was right in 2 Samuel 2:4–7.

Remember that you are not destined for the earth only; you have a celestial destination, where you will remain for eternity in the presence of the Lord. Remember also that the end is already written. Satan is not the winner. Focus on this, and your perspective will be transformed, even in challenging times. Learn to stand.

WALK BY FAITH EVERY DAY

"So David sent messengers to the men of Jabesh-Gilead, and said to them:

> 'You are blessed of the Lord, for you have shown this kindness to your Lord, to Saul, and have buried him. And now may the Lord show kindness and truth to you. I will also repay you for this kindness, because you have done this thing. Now therefore, let your hands be strengthened, and be valiant; for your master Saul is

dead, and also the house of Judah has anointed me king over them'" (2 Samuel 2:4–7).

REFLECTION QUESTIONS

Take a moment to reflect on your life today. Did you let discouragement creep in, or is it still very close? What steps can you take to overcome it and regain your freedom? What choices can you make today to prevent finding yourself in this situation again?

How can the gift of wisdom help you and your family in your everyday life?

PART 3

Those Who Walked with God

Illustration 3: Enoch

Only two people did not know death in the Bible: Enoch and Elijah. Even Abraham, who was called a friend of God (and he is the only one to ever received this name officially) died of old age. King David, who was a man according to God's own heart (and he is the only one to ever received this name officially too), died of old age. It takes a very special kind of relationship to be taken while still alive. For Enoch, he walked with God.

ENOCH

Reading: Genesis 5:21–24 and Jude v. 14

It takes a very particular kind of person for God to choose to be taken and not know death, knowing that death is a curse imposed on the world and every living thing. Enoch's life was different from everyone else's. It is said that he walked with God. He was the only one in the entire Bible to receive this attribute.

Not much is known about Enoch. His biography consists of three verses in the book of Genesis and a few verses in the book of Jude. Yet, amid a genealogy of thirty-two verses, the author of the book of Genesis pauses to note the characteristics of this man's life. Enoch means "consecrated" in Hebrew, so he was consecrated from birth and followed this path throughout his life. Enoch is the son of Jared and the father of Methuselah, whom he had at the age of sixty-five. He is also Noah's great-grandfather. Born into a family worshipping the Lord, he was the seventh after Adam.

Along with Elijah, he is the only man to have been raptured before experiencing death, a privilege that was not granted to Moses, Isaiah, or the apostles. Enoch's life, therefore, must have been pleasing to God. Although it was shorter than everyone else's at the time (365 years), his life had a profound influence on those who came after him: among his descendants were Methuselah and Noah. Methuselah lived for 969 years. A calculation tells us that Methuselah died in the year of the Flood. Enoch's faithfulness to God, his decision to walk with Him and not follow the trends of society, had a lasting impact on his descendants because it is also written that Noah was found to be a man of integrity, probably due to the teachings he received from his ancestors. This illustrates the power of faith and its ability to shape future generations.

Enoch walked with God for three hundred years after his son's birth. He also lived three generations before Noah. We know the state of society in Noah's day since the Lord had decided to destroy mankind through a flood, saving only Enoch's great-grandson and his family. This means that Enoch witnessed the gradual degradation of society. In Noah's day, there were no priests; man could have a direct relationship with the Lord. To walk with the Lord is to speak with Him, to do what is right in His sight when all others decide to do what pleases them. So, the Lord had the kind of relationship and communication with him that He wanted to have from the beginning with Adam and Eve. The reader tends to overlook "walked with God" as a notion lost amid a genealogy. But this expression deserves to be dwelt upon because Enoch, thanks to his faithfulness, did not know death. One day, "he was no more, because the Lord took him" (Genesis 5:24). The event must have become a legend and a part of this family's stories. Noah was four years old when Enoch was taken. We don't know if he was caught up in a whirlwind like Elijah or if it was a quiet, unnoticed event, but we do know that it was an event that marked this family and impacted the people of later generations through Noah.

Enoch was also a prophet: the name Methuselah means "that which shall be sent at his death" ("The Man of the Arrow" or "the Man Who Was Sent"). Given the progressive degradation of society, Enoch had received a warning from God that something would happen when his son died, and he named his son to become a sign for future generations. Methuselah lived a long time, 969 years. The Lord has been patient with humans, warning them for almost a millennium. Enoch also received a prophecy and a vision of the Last Judgment: This prophecy is found in Jude 14:15: "For them also Enoch, the seventh since Adam, prophesied, saying, 'Behold, the Lord has come with his holy myriads, to exercise judgment against all, and to make all the ungodly among them give an account of all the ungodly deeds they have committed, and of all the evil words that sinners have spoken against him ungodly.'" For them, verse 14, refers to the men mentioned in verse 4 of the book of Jude: some ungodly men "who turn the grace of our God into dissolution, and deny our only Master and Lord Jesus Christ" (Jude 1:4). Enoch's generation behaved in this manner; they had renounced their ties with God, and Enoch was the voice that announced the coming judgment if the people did not repent. Not only did Enoch warn the people of his generation, but he also conveyed his message to future generations through the name he gave his son. This prophecy serves as a reminder to us, the readers, that we should not turn away from God's grace and that we should always be prepared for the Day of Judgment.

In conclusion, from Enoch's life and testimony, we draw four lessons. First, don't choose sin or let corruption get into the heart, much like Adam and Eve before the Fall. Walk with God every day, in His presence and wisdom. It will save you from many pitfalls and traps and guide you in your everyday decision-making. The Holy Spirit will warn you when there is danger. You will know true peace and be guided in decision-making. But don't forget to teach and model this determination to your children, your family, your friends, and all those who gravitate around you.

Second, understand that your actions and decisions have repercussions for generations. Your life continues to influence those who come after you, even after you are gone. In my family, we still talk about our grandparents' testimonies and faithfulness when facing tribulations and tough choices, in particular during World War II. Some post-modern philosophies suggest that everything we do won't matter in a few years. Enoch proves us wrong; his descendants included Noah and all his family. They all were saved from the Flood.

Third, the life of Enoch teaches us that it is still possible to walk with God and that God rejoices in seeing men and women choose to live according to His precepts, despite the general trends. "How do I walk with God?" you might ask. First, it's a personal and internal decision, one made through prayer, communication with the Holy Spirit, contemplation, and a study of the Word. Next, align your values with those of the Lord, and resist sin with the help and guidance of the Holy Spirit. Third, use discernment and listen to the warnings. Spend time with Him. Go on prayer walk, build a prayer room or closet in your house, and pray with your family, for your friends.

Finally, Methuselah's longevity reminds us that the Lord still has patience with His people and that "He wills that all men should be saved" (1 Timothy 2:4). Let's pass along this message and leave a lasting impact on those who will come after us. Testimony, prayer, donations to support ministries, etc., are the standards by which you can participate in building the Kingdom of God.

WALK BY FAITH EVERY DAY

"And Enoch walked with God; and he was not, for God took him" (Genesis 5:24).

REFLECTION QUESTIONS

Consider Enoch, his walk with God, his legacy, and his message. How can you impact the future generations today? What type of legacy do you want to leave your children and their children after them? What can you do, today, to work on that legacy?

PART 4

Those Who Trusted God

Illustration 4: The Samaritan Woman

A lot of things in the Bible point toward trusting the Lord with all our needs: tithing, the Sabbath, the Jubilee every forty-nine years, etc. The question these ask is: Will we trust the Lord with our lives, our finances, our families in good or difficult times? The widow of Zarephath and the shepherds are here to encourage us to trust God and make Him part of our lives.

THE WIDOW OF ZAREPHATH

Sometimes, serving God can be perceived as controversial by the world because it contradicts current cultural or philosophical trends. Few women in the Bible were as contentious as the widow of Zarephath, who hosted Elijah during the drought narrated in 1 Kings 17. After all, even the people of Nazareth were furious at Jesus when He spoke about her (Luke 4:23–27).

1 Kings 17 narrates the story of a drought that happened in Israel. This was the very drought the prophet Elijah had declared to compel King Ahab to heed the Lord. Toward the middle of this drought, the prophet found himself in need as his supernatural resources were exhausted: The water from the

brook Cherith had dried up, and the crows stopped bringing food. Elijah had to move.

Interestingly, the Lord found a widow in Zarephath, a non-Israelite territory near Sidon, a woman of minimal means and no significance, to become Elijah's protector. Just as the Lord commanded the crows to feed Elijah for a time, He also instructed the Sidonian woman to supply Elijah's needs for an extended period.

Although the woman's name is still unknown, her actions speak volumes. We know very little about her. She was a Phoenician of a village near the town of Sidon, so she was a Sidonian, a lady raised in the same beliefs, culture, and religion as Jezebel, then the queen of Israel, wife of King Ahab. The very same queen who brought the cult of Baal to Israel, who fed the false prophets at her table every day. So, this widow was the enemy of everything Elijah stood for. Add to this that this woman had probably heard of a bounty placed on Elijah a little while earlier, and the death sentence over his head, and all who would help him[5]. Let's add to this that she was a widow. In this time and place, widows were amongst the most vulnerable members of society, left without the protection and the provision of their husbands. She depended entirely on the goodwill of her husband's family, which did not care much, apparently, since she was left to gather sticks by herself, and with no food or oil to survive. Moreover,

---

5   In 1 Kings 18:9–14, Elijah meets Obadiah (Ahab's palace administrator) who says that if he were to go and tell the king he had found Elijah, he would be put to death.

she had a son for whom she was responsible. So, with no means, no resources, and a household to feed during a drought, in human eyes, she was not the ideal candidate to take care of a mighty prophet of God.

However, she agreed to give everything she had to the man of God. When Elijah first met her, he asked for water. Remember that Israel and the surrounding lands had been experiencing a severe drought for some time. There had been no rain for a year and a half already, so the wells were likely very low or even dry. Still, she agreed to provide water to the man of God. Then, he asked her to cook food. He didn't say to cook and share; he asked to cook for him first, then for her son and herself. During a drought, the harvest was probably poor—no cereals, no olives, no wheat, no fruits, no food. Yet, she agreed to this, demonstrating her faith and trust in God's provision.

Among all the people in Israel, none was found worthy or trusty enough to become host to the prophet, so the Lord found a widow from a foreign nation to fulfill His will. Despite the potential danger, the widow courageously sheltered and fed the most wanted man in Israel and Phoenicia. Her bravery went beyond mere protection, surpassing even that of Obadiah, who was fearful when he met Elijah (1 Kings 18:9–14). She kept the man of God in her house, a testament to her courage.

However, the author of 1 Kings says that she went, cooked bread for the prophet, but that as she went on cooking, the flour did not diminish in the pot, nor did the oil go dry "…she and her household ate for many days" (1 Kings 17:15). She followed

Elijah's directions. She saw the promise become reality (1 Kings 17:14). When she went to cook, she shut the door of her house. By closing the door to doubt and choosing to do what was right in God's eyes, the widow demonstrated her faith. In response, the Lord first honored her faith by providing a miracle, and then by answering Elijah's prayers and bringing her son back to life when he died.

What can we learn from this woman? First, God can use anyone available, even the least expected: a donkey, crows, or, in this case, an enemy. Obedience is more important than sacrifices, and faith is the only thing that impressed Jesus Christ while He was on Earth. The widow's obedience, even in the face of scarcity and danger, serves as a powerful example for everyone.

Second, life is challenging. Family may abandon you, the world might turn against you, or you could find yourself alone facing a difficult situation. Know that the Lord will never leave or forsake you, no matter what comes your way, if you stay in Him and trust Him. When addressing Elijah, the widow said, "As surely as the Lord your God lives" (1 Kings 17:12). The Lord is not yet her God, but she knows of Him and recognizes that Elijah is His prophet. She is already beginning to develop a fear of the Lord.

How will you respond to what comes your way? The widow's reaction to the drought and King Ahab's response are complete opposites: The widow found salvation by accepting the Lord's representative in her house. Ahab rejected and rebelled against the Word of God and His prophet, threatening, refusing to listen, and resisting the necessary changes that could improve everyone's life. Ahab knew the solution: Elijah told him there would be no water except at his word. How will you respond when facing tough times? You are the master of your choices and actions. Will you be like Ahab or the widow?

Understand the Word of God and keep it safe in your house and your heart. Elijah moved into her house and stayed there until it was time for him to appear before King Ahab. When everyone was suffering from the drought, the widow had food and oil to care for her son, the prophet, and herself. She lived in the miraculous for months. When her son died, she called upon the prophet, who brought her son back to life through divine intervention.

Close your door to doubt, fear, and the noises of the world. Focus on the Lord, pray, and spend time with Him in your house. Rely on His goodness to care for you.

Since this woman was considered insignificant, abandoned by her family and community, she became an extension of God's hand, bringing change and safety to Elijah. She became the embodiment and demonstration of God's goodness to the prophet. Jesus referenced her story when He spoke in the synagogue of Nazareth to emphasize that even non-Jews can find favor in God's eyes and that God looks beyond appearances to the heart.

WALK BY FAITH EVERY DAY

"Trust in the Lord with all your heart,
And lean not on your own understanding;
In all your ways acknowledge Him,
And He shall direct your paths" (Proverbs 3:5–6).

REFLECTION QUESTIONS

When fear and doubt come knocking at your door, what can you do to make them go away? Think of different ways you can use the Word of God to keep you in trusting God and walking in faith.

Also, how can you make a difference in those around you and embody God's goodness for both believers and non-believers today?

THE SHEPHERDS

Reading: Luke 2:8-19

When God needs to deliver a message to us, He looks for someone available. Whom He finds might be unexpected. At the start of the Gospel of Luke, between 4 and 6 AD, God chose to reveal His glory and His plan of salvation to all the people living in Judea. After all, a star shone in the sky for a long time when Jesus was born[6]. The only people He found available at that time were a group of shepherds. No one else was free to pay attention, as everyone was busy returning to their hometowns to be registered for the Quirinius census. Out in the fields, away from the city, watching their sheep, the shepherds spend their

______

6   There is no set time regarding the actual time the star shone. However, scholars estimate that the star shone between a few months up to two years. The Gospel of Matthew explains that the Magi's journey from the East probably lasted two years to complete since Herod ordered the killing of all the baby boys two and under.

summers and falls under the stars in reflection. While living with their sheep and apart from civilization, the shepherds lead a life of solitude and sacrifice, tending to the weakest and most helpless animals. Gathering around the campfire at night, their hearts were open to receiving the Good News. In this time of silence and contemplation, the first angel came to announce the birth of Jesus Christ. Soon after the initial contact, other angels joined in a "multitude of heavenly hosts praising God" (Luke 2:13). What a sight it might have been for these shepherds!

Because their hearts were open, they were the first to receive the revelation of God coming as a man. As the Bible says, God reveals Himself to the humble but confounds the proud (James 4:6). This event happened soon after Jesus' birth, when they found Him still in the manger. It is also written that they told Joseph and Mary everything they had seen and heard regarding the newborn. Joseph and Mary probably needed reassurance. They had just become parents outside of marriage, with nowhere to go; no one wanted to take them in, and they likely faced difficult times until they were officially married. So, the shepherds were sent as God's messengers. They became the carriers of God's voice and promises. Mary kept their words in her heart; she "treasured all these things, pondering them in her heart" (Luke 2:19). Their words made a significant impact on Mary and Joseph that lasted.

Keep your heart and eyes open, turned toward the Lord. The possibilities are endless for Him. God reveals Himself to those who take the time to seek Him and stay in His presence. Today, in a highly connected world, learn to tune out the voices of the city: the yelling of politics, the dramatic events, the economic turmoil, and the discouraging news. Set yourselves apart to hear the voice of the Lord, the angels singing, and to share the message of the Gospel with those around you who are weary, tired, or in need of a blessing.

Turn off the noise of the world for a moment. Our minds are constantly bombarded with novel ideas, the news, and economic and political uncertainties. Take a moment to contemplate the Creation and meditate on God's greatness. Let God handle the big things. Bring encouragement to those who are tired and weary, and be the bearer of Good News: salvation and eternal life. You can make a difference.

WALK BY FAITH EVERY DAY

"But those who wait on the Lord
Shall renew their strength;
They shall mount up with wings like eagles,
They shall run and not be weary,
They shall walk and not faint" (Isaiah 40:31).

REFLECTION QUESTIONS

What can you do today to be more attentive to the voice of the Lord? What steps can you take to hear His voice again?

THE SAMARITAN WOMAN

Reading: John 4

John 4 is the only Gospel to narrate the conversion of a Samaritan woman, whose name is not mentioned, and the revival that followed her testimony in Sychar, Samaria. This timely encounter between Jesus Christ and the woman at the well, and the revelation that followed, surprised everyone. From the disciples to the town's inhabitants, passing by the woman herself, all were left dumbfounded by Jesus Christ's actions and words because what He kept hidden from the other Jews, speaking in parables, He revealed to her, a Samaritan and a woman: the Kingdom to come, the worship to come, the life to come. In a sense, she foreshadowed the coming spread of the Gospel to non-Jews and its universal reach: all can get saved. However, they must first repent and change their lives.

The story begins with Jesus, who was on His way from Galilee to Judea, walking across Samaria, near the town of Sychar. Tired and thirsty, He sits alone by the well of Jacob outside the village of Sychar because He sent His disciples to purchase groceries in the nearby city. As He is sitting, waiting, a woman arrives. This woman came to Jacob's well early in the morning to avoid the crowd and the heat of the sun. Some say it was late at night. In any case, she was trying to pass unnoticed. But as we know, those who nobody notices or that everybody tries to avoid, but who are looking for the truth deep in their heart, will get noticed by Jesus Christ. It is written that the Samaritan woman had had five husbands and that the last companion she lived with was not her husband. Was she a widow? Had she been repudiated? Was she cursed? Either she was not lucky in her choices of a marital mate, or she had made some bad decisions that led her to become a double outcast by social and ethnic standards. She was living with a man who was not her husband (which, according to Mosaic Law was punishable by death), and she was an outcast among outcasts because all Samaritans were considered impure by the Jews for historical reasons.

As she approaches the well, Jesus begins a conversation with her on the topic of her life, surprising her for multiple reasons. First, she was a Samaritan, and as such had no relations or communications with Jews because of ancestral disagreements.

Second, she was alone, she was a woman, and He was a man talking to her. Talk about breaking social barriers! The more we hide from human eyes, the more we attract the Lord's eyes.

This encounter is significant for multiple reasons. Let's analyze the Samaritan woman's side first. To go to the well, she had to exit the four walls of the house that protected her from the crowd. She had to leave the safety of the barriers she had built to prevent an invasion that could potentially change her life. As we later discover during the conversation, she had been living in sin, hidden from everyone. But she left her house to go to the desert out of necessity, and there she met Jesus. Following this encounter, the one who had wanted to live hidden away from the crowd returned to the crowd to spread the Good News. Her transformation from a sinner to a fearless evangelist is a powerful testimony to the transformative love of Jesus. All fears were gone; her sin had been exposed to the light, and she had nothing to hide anymore. She received the revelation of who Jesus was. She asked all the questions she had on her mind and didn't hide anything. She was ultimately open because Jesus had broken down the barriers of prejudice and pride that divided and did not unite.

The Samaritan woman received the revelation of who the Messiah was from the mouth of the Messiah Himself. She also received the revelation of true worship and the revelation of salvation. That's a lot of revelations for one person, especially when considering that no one else, except the disciples, received clear answers. The one who came to get water to keep became the source of the water itself. Jesus shared the same message with the Jews while in Jerusalem (?) in John 7:37–38. However, unlike the Samaritan woman, they rejected Him. By going to the village and spreading the news that she had met the Messiah, she demonstrated exactly what Jesus told her: Living waters sprang forth from her, and she shared life with those she feared, without fear.

What can we learn from her testimony?

Today, Jesus sits and waits for us to come and receive His living water. Those who are thirsty for truth, justice, and peace will always get life-changing answers from Jesus if they engage in the conversation and listen to his message. They are invited to ask honest and sincere questions. His answers will bring life to those who listen because His Word is the Life, He is the Life.

Today, you are the bearer of the Good News, the Gospel, a message that can save, change, deliver, and set free from sin and Satan's grip. Fear is a tactic Satan uses to discourage and spread chaos among the Lord's army. Do not fear, bring to light Satan's lies and tactics. He is *like* a roaring lion, but he is not the lion. Jesus Christ is the Lion of Judah.

Society will try to make you fit into boxes and classes, and outcast you for whatever reason it will find if you refuse to follow its trends. This is particularly true, especially if you are a disciple of Jesus Christ. However, know that when the world is coming against you, Jesus will stand by your side, speaking words of life and light, giving you revelation after revelation if you remain near Him and live by His law. When you hear the message of the Good News, abandon sin and walk in the freedom that Jesus offers.

Don't keep the message for yourself. That freedom you experienced when you first met Jesus Christ, share it with the ones around you. The Samaritan woman's role as a messenger of the Gospel is a powerful reminder of the urgency and importance of evangelism. Some will listen; others will not. Still, spread it and the Holy Spirit will do the rest.

To conclude the story of the Samaritan woman, after she returned to the village and shared what had happened with the other Samaritans, they all came to listen to Jesus, and many were saved. The words of one woman, touched and transformed by truth, brought revival in her community.

WALK BY FAITH EVERY DAY

Jesus answered and said to her, "If you knew the gift of God, and who it is who says to you, 'Give Me a drink,' you would have asked Him, and He would have given you living water… Jesus answered and said to her, 'Whoever drinks of this water will thirst again, but whoever drinks of the water that I shall give him will never thirst. But the water that I shall give him will become in him a fountain of water springing up into everlasting life'" (John 4:10–14).

REFLECTION QUESTIONS

Reflect on the transformation that happened in the Samaritan woman after she met Jesus Christ and heard the truth. What did you feel, experience, or understand when you first came in contact with the Gospel? How did you change? What can you do today to, like this woman, change other people's lives?

PART 5

Those Who Did Not Fear Man

Illustration 5: Joash

Fear is a tactic used to paralyze an opponent and defeat him. Satan uses fear to defeat the soldiers in the Lord's army. However, tradition says that the phrase "Do not fear" is found 365 times in the Bible. Every day, the Lord tells us not to fear. The Bible also gives us examples of men and women who did not fear man: Rahab, the prostitute; Joash, Gideon's father; the Samaritan woman; and Shobi, Machir, and Barzillai are some examples we can learn from.

RAHAB

Reading: Joshua 2, and 6:22-25

As Joshua and the Hebrews prepared to enter and conquer the Promised Land, they reached their first stop after crossing the Jordan River: the city of Jericho. Jericho became the first test of faith for the Hebrews. The defensive walls surrounding Jericho were a classic example of city fortifications. They were so thick that they housed the homes of part of the population, usually the poorest or those with a bad reputation. As the Hebrews faced this stronghold, would they trust the Lord, or would they lose courage? We know the Lord commanded Joshua to be strong and courageous in the first chapter of the book that bears his name (Joshua 1:8). However, He also used other means to show He would be with His people, sometimes through unexpected sources. In Jericho's case, the spies found safety in the house of a woman of ill repute. God is not short of ways to catch our attention.

Rahab was a woman who used her body to make a living, an activity forbidden by the Lord in the Mosaic Law (Leviticus 19:29 and Deuteronomy 23:18–19). Prostitution was viewed differently in the Canaanite pagan culture, which saw prostitutes and prostitution in general as ways to ensure the fertility of the land and its inhabitants. Still, Rahab the prostitute made a choice that affected her life, the Hebrews' future, and attracted the Lord's attention: She saved the lives of the two Hebrew spies, sent by Joshua, from perversion and destruction by her fellow city dwellers. Because the Lord found her willing and ready to change her ways and serve the Hebrews, because she took a stand for what was right—not in her own eyes, nor the eyes of the culture she grew up in, but in the Lord's—and because she feared the Lord, she found herself in a position to bargain for her salvation and that of her family members.

So, how did she make a difference, and what does it mean for us?

By welcoming the two men into her house, she allowed representatives and members of God's people to enter, thereby allowing the truth and power of God to settle in her home. The story continues that the king of Jericho decided to kill, or maybe worse (we remember Sodom), the two Hebrew men who were staying in Rahab's house. By protecting the two spies, Rahab stood against the king of Jericho, who sent men to capture them. She protected the two men by directing the king's envoys in the wrong direction, sending them far away from her house and the Hebrews. When the members of God's people arrived, she switched her spiritual allegiance. As mentioned earlier, in Canaanite cultures and other pagan religions, prostitutes were agents of fertility deities such as Asherah and Baal, and the act of prostitution was sacred. It was considered a service to the community. Through ritual sexual holy rites in the deities' temples, they aimed to ensure an abundant crop harvest and fertility among people and animals. However, she gave up this practice and belief to follow the Lord and was later blessed. Matthew 1:5 says that she married a Hebrew man named Salmon; she had a son, Boaz, who married another Canaanite woman, Ruth. And, as we know, Ruth was the great-grandmother of King David.

After giving up the culture she grew up in, in chapter 2:9–11, it is written that she recognized the Lord as God, switching allegiance, and encouraged the two men by narrating all the great deeds of the Lord for the Hebrews. She says in verse 10: "For we have heard how the Lord dried up the water of the Red Sea for you when you came out of Egypt, and what you did to the two kings of the Amorites who were on the other side of the Jordan, Sihon and Og, whom you utterly destroyed." Out of all the people in Jericho, who knew of the Hebrews and their God, she was the only one who feared and chose the Lord. The king of Jericho and his men decided to fight against them and resist. She confessed the Lord. Talking to the men, hidden on her roof, she says in Joshua 2 v. 11: "And as soon as we heard these things, our hearts melted; neither did there remain any more courage in anyone because of you, for the Lord your God, He is God in heaven above and on earth beneath." Truth travels, so does the renown of the Lord. His power and greatness preceded the Hebrews, preparing the way for them to conquer the land. Rahab says, "When we heard of it, our hearts melted in fear, and everyone's courage failed because of you," in Joshua 2:11. It is one thing to have heard of the Lord; it is another to know Him. Don't settle for just learning about the Lord, but come to know Him and proclaim Him as master over your life, as God over Heaven and Earth.

Additionally, after showing her goodwill and true repentance, she negotiated with the two men for her own protection and that of her family, including her father, mother, brothers, sisters, and all those who belonged to them (chapter 2: 12–13). She secured a promise of salvation for all.

Last, she acted on the Lord's words: She attached the scarlet cord to her window and was saved from destruction just like all those who put blood on their doors while in Egypt were saved on the night that the angel of destruction passed through the streets (Exodus 12:23).

In today's world, amid rising chaos, as Rahab did, we will eventually have to choose our civic allegiance. When faced with the truth and the Lord, we will be required to make a decision. Are we on the side of God or Satan? There is no in-between. Rejecting the king's orders, Rahab switched her allegiance from Jericho to the Hebrews and proved it by putting her life at risk. She became a traitor to her people, which was likely considered a severe crime, potentially punishable by death or worse.

Rahab's testimony still speaks today. In the same way that you choose a civic allegiance, you must also choose your spiritual allegiance. Get rid of the sin that plagues your life, start anew with the power to stand, and resist temptations. That's the real freedom. When in doubt or scared or unsure, remind yourself that you serve and belong to the great God who parted the Red Sea. Feed your soul with His Word, bless Him for His wondrous deeds, and remember all the miracles you witnessed or heard of. Don't focus on your limitations and circumstances; turn your eyes upon Jesus and His promises. They are here to build up your faith.

Don't keep salvation to yourself, but share it and ask for the salvation of your people, and plead the blood of Jesus over your life. The scarlet cord attached to the window played the same role as the blood on the doorposts back in Egypt. As death passed through the streets of Jericho after the walls were destroyed, Rahab and all those in her house were spared and welcomed among God's people. As this world slowly descends into chaos, your house will become a place of safety because it is under the Lord's protection. You will become a stronghold that others will find refuge in, and be restored to life through your faith. Make your life changes visible; display your allegiance at your metaphorical window. The Lord will be with you; He will protect you. This is His promise.

In conclusion, it does not matter where you are right now or what you do. If the truth comes knocking at your door, let it in, allow it to change your life, and those of all your people. Protect it like a treasure. Cast away sin, repent, and declare your allegiance to the Lord through your words and behavior. The Lord will take care of you from the sinful swamps and fortresses of Jericho, and you will enter the Promised Land. Without Rahab, we would have never read about the fall of Jericho, the conquest of the Promised Land. There would be no King David, no King Solomon, no Joseph, the earthly father of Jesus Christ.

WALK BY FAITH EVERY DAY

"If we confess our sins, He is faithful and just to forgive us *our* sins and to cleanse us from all unrighteousness" (1 John 1:9).

REFLECTION QUESTIONS

Consider your present situation. Are you like Rahab, captive in the walls of Satan, or is your house a haven and a refuge where the Lord reigns? Place yourself and all those of your household under the blood of Jesus Christ and the Lord's protection, and your influence will grow. What can you do today to increase this influence and transform the situations of those around you? Remember, the power of truth is in your hands.

JOASH

An angry crowd is scary. An angry religious crowd is terrifying.

Among the great warriors and leaders of the Old Testament is Gideon, a little man with an extensive complex of the small. However, few realize that without his father's intervention, there would be no Gideon story, and Israel would not have known the great victory that followed.

After the Lord freed Israel from Egyptian control under Moses' leadership, He made a covenant with them. One of the laws stated that the Lord was the only God they should worship:

> You shall not make idols for yourselves;
> Neither a carved image nor a sacred pillar shall you rear
> up for yourselves;

> Nor shall you set up an engraved stone in your land to bow down to it;
>
> For I am the Lord your God (Leviticus 26:1).

However, soon after the Israelites settled in the Promised Land (Canaan), Israel adopted the customs and religion of the local Canaanite groups, including idol worship, thus openly rebelling against the Lord's laws. Israel angered the Lord and faced the consequences of its rebellion: as He promised in Leviticus 26, the Lord sent Madian, Amalek, and the Sons of the Orient to invade and attack Israel repeatedly. They destroyed crops (Judges 6:4), stole cattle (Judges 6:4), and seized all the food reserves (Judges 6:4). They settled with tents "as numerous as locusts" (Judges 6:5).

So, the situation in Israel during the period of the Judges was far from idyllic.

However, the consequences were not meant to last forever. The Lord delivered Israel many times through brave men and heroes. That's where Gideon and Joash come in. Gideon was Joash's son, an Israelite from the tribe of Manasseh, who, like everyone else, had strayed from the God of Israel and embraced the local religion. He worshipped Baal and had built an altar to this god on his property, with a sacred pole on top dedicated to Asherah, the mother goddess. All aspects of this religion were offensive to the Lord. Baal was the male fertility god, one of the main deities in the Canaanite pantheon, bearing titles such as *Prince* and *Lord of the Earth*. He was also the god of sowing and harvest. Dagon, the idol that fell before the Ark of the Covenant in 1 Samuel 5, was his father. On top of that, you can imagine that the fertility cult linked with Baal involved behaviors disapproved by the Lord. The worship of Baal was very sensual and often included sacred prostitutes in or near temples. Sometimes, it also involved human sacrifices and wild rites of self-mutilation, like those described in 1 Kings 18:28 on Mount Carmel. Additionally, the Bible clearly shows that Joash was very dedicated to this god: The altar was so large that two bulls and ten servants were needed to dismantle it.

Happily for us, the story does not end there. After dismantling the altar, the crowd came and knocked on Joash's door, demanding Gideon's death for what he had done. Joash stood bravely between his son and those who wanted to kill him. This act of courage allowed Gideon to raise an army and deliver Israel from their enemies. After this great victory, Gideon became a judge in Israel, and peace was restored for a long time.

What can we learn from Joah's intervention, and how did he make a difference?

First, Joash's house illustrates how idols can destroy our lives. Idols can sneak in if we're not careful: work, TV, money, relationships, social media, reputation—idols come in many forms. Once they take hold, they are very hard to remove. The longer they stay, the bigger they grow, the more space they take up, and the more attention they demand. Satan won't give up his rights without a fight.

Second, Gideon grew up hearing about the wonders of the past from his father, which is why he said, "O my Lord, if the Lord is with us, why then has all this happened to us? And where are all His miracles which our fathers told us about, saying, 'Did not the Lord bring us up from Egypt?' But now the Lord has forsaken us and handed us over to the Midianites." A remnant of the past still lingered. Yet, the Israelites no longer knew the Lord and had forgotten His laws, as they worshipped other gods. Like Joash and the Israelites, one can know about the Lord but not follow His commands. Knowing about the Lord is not enough.

Third, Joash, the owner of the shrine, likely witnessed what happened during the night. After all, they all lived under the same roof. Gideon knew the risks of tearing down this altar. He was fearful and acted at night. Of course, the next morning, the crowd was offended by Gideon's actions. They came to Joash's doorstep demanding reparation, intent on taking Gideon out and killing him: "Then the men of the city said to Joash, 'Bring out your son, that he may die, because he has torn down the altar of Baal, and because he has cut down the wooden image that was beside it'" (Judges 6:30). However, this angry religious crowd did not get the response they expected. Instead, Joash's reaction was completely the opposite. It left the crowd perplexed, and they left without harming Gideon. In fact, instead of giving his son to the crowd or bowing to the idol, he took a stand and challenged Baal to defend himself, threatening those who would stand for Baal: "Would you plead for Baal? Would you save him? Let the one who would plead for him be put to death by morning! If he is a god, let him plead for himself, because his altar has been torn down!" Something changed in Joash's heart that night as the idols came down. Whatever that was, it changed him, turning him from an idol worshipper into a devoted soldier of God. He stood bravely in front of a furious crowd. He was truly transformed.

Fourth, taking a stand with words is one thing. Following words with action is another. As Gideon hid in fear inside the house, Joash stepped forward and placed himself between the crowd and his son, fearless, like Elijah on Mount Carmel. At that moment, as Joash stands before the crowd for truth and God, he is no longer a representative of the weakest clan in Manasseh (Judges 6:15). He is clothed with authority from above, an authority that will influence the crowd, who will later respond *en masse* to Gideon's call for battle: 32,000 men will answer (Judges 7:3). By standing against the crowd, Joash took a stand against bullies. He acted courageously when the moment called for it. He remained fearless, confronting lies and deceit with the truth. Everyone witnessed the change happening in a former worshipper of Baal.

Joash's words made a profound impact on the Israelites, and after his speech, Gideon was given a new name. He became known as Jerubbaal after Joash said, "If he is a god, let him plead for himself." These words echoed in the ears and minds of the people.

How can Joash inspire us today?

Idols have no place in our homes. We worship the Lord, the Almighty God, the Lord of Hosts, and Him alone. Idols, whether moral, physical, or spiritual, should be removed from our lives and families. They are open doors to worse curses, bondage, and fear. If we leave a crack in the door, Satan will run through it and settle. Just as Gideon destroyed the altar and the pole and built an altar to the true God, we must cleanse our homes of everything offensive to Him. Every idol must be eliminated. Gideon had to take down everything as a sign of obedience and a test; since he was called to serve the Lord, he had to lead a small expedition before leading a larger one and sever ties with generational alliances and curses. Joash was transformed when all sight of idols was removed. He was set free and reminded of to whom his allegiance belonged. Baal's altar and the pole of Ashera were only wood and bricks.

Simply knowing the Lord or relying on past alliances isn't enough. God desires people who seek a personal relationship with Him to honestly know Him and live according to His law, which frees them from sin. He searches for soldiers who will stand bravely for Him when the time comes, serving in His army with confidence that they are not alone in the fight.

In one night, Joash transformed from a servant to Satan and his demons into a soldier in the Lord's army who stood against the multitude. He was on the frontlines so that Gideon could finish the work he was called to do later.

There are no further mentions of Joash after these events. He fades into the shadows of history, passing the platform to his son. Humility goes hand in hand with service.

Like Joash's, may our words resonate and mark the people to the point of changing the identity of those around us. May our words be few but life-changing and impactful. May our words be worthy of being remembered as our legacy, and may our behavior positively impact those who surround us as well.

May change be visible and trigger the same in those who see and hear us. Fear is the strongest motivator. It is stronger even than the perspective of happiness. May the fear of the Lord overpower the fear of man.

False gods are illusions. We belong to the one true God.

WALK BY FAITH EVERY DAY

"Fear not, for I am with you;
Be not dismayed, for I am your God.
I will strengthen you,
Yes, I will help you,
I will uphold you with
My righteous right hand" (Isaiah 41:10).

REFLECTION QUESTIONS

Take a moment to reflect on your life as it is today. Do you have idols that prevent you from spending more time with the Lord? What do you think could happen if you were to remove these idols and replace them with the worship of the Lord? What can you do today to change this situation?

SHOBI, MACHIR, AND BARZILLAI

Reading: 2 Samuel 17:27, 2 Samuel 19:31–39, 1 Kings 2:7

As King David neared the end of his life, he faced perhaps the most arduous battle of his reign against a fierce and unrelenting enemy: his son, Absalom. Humiliated publicly, a victim of a *coup d'état,* and forced to leave Jerusalem with his family, court, and men, King David saw his demise approaching as the people of Israel turned against him. He crossed the Jordan River, leaving everything behind and admitting defeat. Even the Israelites on the west bank of the Jordan River, who had acclaimed and crowned him king, chose to follow the handsome, proud, and rebellious self-proclaimed king, Absalom.

Despite the overwhelming odds, God showed His mercy and goodness to David. Everything seemed over and lost for David.

Crossing the Jordan River was a form of admission of defeat and surrender for the king, as he was no longer present to rule the land. However, it was also a form of surrender to the Lord. As he was leaving Jerusalem, he ordered Zadok and Abiathar to return the Ark of the Covenant to Jerusalem, saying: "If I find favor in the sight of the Lord, then He will bring me back again and show me both it and His habitation. But if He should say thus, 'I have no delight in you,' behold, here I am, let Him do to me as seems good to Him" (2 Samuel 15:25–26). So, David and his people passed the brook Kidron, the Jordan River, and entered the wilderness. That's where the Lord met David. He met him on the other side of the river, in the wilderness, through the selfless generosity of three men: Shobi, the son of Nahash from Rabbah of the sons of Ammon; Machir, the son of Ammiel from Lo-debar; and Barzillai the Gileadite from Regelim. These men, without any personal gain in mind, provided David with everything necessary to survive in a new place. Their generosity knew no bounds, as they brought "beds, basins, pottery, wheat, barley, flour, parched grain, beans, lentils, parched seeds, honey, curds, sheep, and cheese" (2 Samuel 17:28) enough to feed six hundred people plus the soldiers.

The loyalty of the men teaches us that first, we see the Lord provides even whether we find ourselves in the wilderness. Sometimes, He will give supernaturally, as in the case of Elijah, who was fed by ravens. Sometimes, He will do it through the hands of our neighbors, friends, or good-willed strangers. These men became an extension of the Lord's hand.

Second, we learn that it is in the wilderness that the true nature of the heart and the true motivations are revealed. These three men did not know the king firsthand, but they came and gave out of the goodness of their hearts, without expecting anything in return. Following this encounter, restored, King David organized his armies to face Absalom and the rebellion (2 Samuel 18:1–2). These men did not view their wealth as their own, but rather as a means to do good: They blessed those who were cursed (2 Samuel 16:5–13, where Shimei curses David), and comforted the weary.

They did not fear death. Knowing Israel was undergoing a civil war between the king and his son, they did not fear the consequences of choosing the currently defeated side. They stood against Absalom, who had just crossed the Jordan River and entered their land. Imagine what could have happened to them and their families had Absalom defeated David and been crowned king? We remember what King Saul did to the priests of the Lord in Nob who helped David as he was fleeing King Saul's persecutions: They gave consecrated bread and a sword to David and his men, and Saul had them slaughtered. All eighty-five! He struck the city of Nob "with the edge of the sword" (2 Samuel 21 and 22). However, Shobi, Machir, and Barzillai chose the man of God over the man of the people, standing in stark contrast to Absalom's rebellion and self-serving actions. As men of wealth and stature, they became models of integrity and loyalty to the surrounding populations, who eventually followed David and fought for him in 2 Samuel 18. Their actions proved the power of words.

These men made a profound difference because they chose God over appearances when everything seemed lost. They acted following their hearts and consciences, doing what was right in the eyes of the Lord. Their actions were deemed worthy to be recorded in the Bible.

Today, follow their example by blessing those around you who are weary, defeated, or in the wilderness, by keeping your eyes fixed on the Lord, even when everything seems lost. You can walk with others, pray for them, and provide for their needs. Do this as unto the Lord, for that is what truly matters. Like these three men, learn to remain loyal to God and not be dazzled by the beauty and wealth and the strength of the world. In the end, they will disappear. Be generous with your blessings. They are not just for you. Find ways to be creative and bless those around you, whether out of the kindness of your heart or to help a soul in need.

Faith is not demonstrated by words but by actions that bring to life the faith you hold. Show your faith, encourage those around you who struggle, and bring peace in difficult times through prayer, a gift, or a kind gesture. These are times when you can be creative!

WALK BY FAITH EVERY DAY

"Look at the birds of the air, for they neither sow nor reap nor gather into barns; yet your heavenly Father feeds them. Are you not of more value than they? Which of you by worrying can add one cubit to his stature? So why do you worry about clothing?

Consider the lilies of the field, how they grow: they neither toil nor spin; and yet I say to you that even Solomon in all his glory was not arrayed like one of these. Now if God so clothes the grass of the field, which today is, and tomorrow is thrown into the oven, will He not much more clothe you, O you of little faith? Therefore do not worry, saying, 'What shall we eat?' or 'What shall we drink?' or 'What shall we wear?' For after all these things the Gentiles seek. For your heavenly Father knows that you need all these things. But seek first the kingdom of God and His righteousness, and all these things shall be added to you. Therefore do not worry about tomorrow, for tomorrow will worry about its own things. Sufficient for the day is its own trouble" (Matthew 6: 26–34).

REFLECTION QUESTIONS

How can you bless someone today?
How can your faith transition from words to actions?

PART 6

Those Who Put Their Talents and Goods to Serve the Lord

Illustration 6: Asaph

Creativity is a general term that covers a vast array of topics: From visual artistry to cooking, design, music composition, or storytelling. There is really only one true Creator, and that is God. However, because we were made in God's image, we all have in us the capacity to create and design.

The Bible is filled with examples of creative people who used their talents to build the Lord's Kingdom: Bezalel, Oholiab, and Asaph are some examples that can inspire us to do the same.

BEZALEL

Reading: Exodus 31

Among the many who served the Lord was a man of the tribe of Judah named Bezalel. Bezalel was the son of Uri, the grandson of Hur, the very same who held Moses' hands up when Joshua was fighting against the Amalekites (Exodus 31:3).

Bezalel was well-known among the Israelites for his artistic skills and dedication. Because of his devotion to his work, he caught the eye of the Lord, who was searching for a servant among His people to complete an exceptional task: to supervise and build the Tabernacle. It is written that the Lord called him by name to His service. The Lord knew He could entrust him and the men in his service with the construction of the Tabernacle.

The name Bezalel means "in the shadow of God." As his name states, God covered him, and he dwelt under His influence.

When people looked at him, they did not see him but the Lord and the abilities that lay in him. Indeed, he was filled with "the Spirit of God in wisdom, in understanding, in knowledge, and in all manner of workmanship" (Exodus 31:3). His art was an extension and the expression of the Lord's beauty and Creation. For this reason, he became the chief architect of the construction of the Tabernacle.

It is often believed that the arts, such as music, are divine. For Bezalel, this was not a metaphoric statement or belief. His abilities came from the Lord. He was gifted and talented from beginning to end. His abilities covered, but were not limited to, gold, silver, bronze, jewels, wood, and fabric. He could carve, cut, set, melt, mold, sew, design, understand, create from blueprints, lead, train, engrave, and, on top of it, he excelled in tapestry making. This divine origin of his talents should inspire us to recognize and utilize our own God-given abilities for His service.

In Exodus, the Lord gave Moses a blueprint for the future Tent of Meeting, also known as the Tabernacle. This was a portable sanctuary, a place where the Israelites could meet with God. Moses, the leader in charge of guiding and judging the Israelites, had no spare time to take on the construction of the Tabernacle and needed someone to do it. This heavenly blueprint, reproduced in earthly words and material, was a representation of God's holy sanctuary and everything within it (Hebrews 9). As such, the builders had to follow this blueprint to the letter. From the colors of the fabrics to the width of the wooden planks, eleven chapters in Exodus describe the Tabernacle and its construction process.

This work was essential because whoever took charge of the construction was tasked with building the House of the Lord on Earth; in other words, Israel's worship depended on their obedience. This was the House where the Lord met with Israel, where the high priest proceeded to the yearly atonement and daily sacrifices. It was a physical and symbolic representation of the Lord's presence and the glory of God among His people. It was no joke!

Exodus 35:30–35 states that he had apprentices under his supervision. Bezalel understood the construction of the Tabernacle was not to be the work of one man only, so he worked with Oholiab, whom the Lord had placed by him. He trained Oholiab, who was himself a master in carpentry, weaving, and embroidery.

The Tent of Meeting became Bezalel's legacy to Israel for generations to come. His work is a testament to the power of serving the Lord with our talents and leaving a lasting legacy. It influenced and stood as a sign in the eyes of millions of Israelites. This should encourage us to consider the lasting impact of our service to the Lord.

What he built defied weather conditions, time, and attacks. It survived multiple moves, packing and unpacking, desert conditions, bumpy rides, and rodent invasions. It lasted until King Solomon completed the construction of the Temple of

Jerusalem around 957 BC. Mathematically, to estimate the use of the Tabernacle, we must add the following:

> Desert: 40 plus years of wandering
>
> 12 Judges: 360 years of invasions and battles
>
> Saul's reign: 40 years of probable neglect
>
> David's reign: 40 years of use
>
> Solomon's reign: 13 years of use until the dedication of

the temple in Jerusalem.

In total, it has been in use for approximately five hundred years since its construction and implementation. Moreover, the utensils Bezalel made for worship were moved to Persia at the end of the kingdom of Judah; the Ark disappeared in the days of King Hezekiah. Part of the creations lasted the entire duration of the Kingdom of Judah, so an additional 350 years.

What can we deduce about Bezalel's character, and how can we learn from him? In general, God uses those who are willing to serve and present specific characteristics. The first was that his heart was in the right place: Exodus 36:2 says that the hearts of Bezalel and Oholihab were "stirred, to come and do the work." Bezalel was not motivated by selfish aims and gains. All his work was done for free, out of joy for service. Next came obedience. There was no room for poetic or artistic license here. Details had to be followed because the blueprint was from God Himself! "Bezalel, the son of Uri, the son of Hur, of the tribe of Judah, made all that the Lord has commanded Moses" (Exodus 38:22). Discipline was a watchword in this service. Third came the dedication to work and duty: He received no pay for his service in constructing the Tabernacle. Honesty comes next in line. The incense used in the Tabernacle was unique and could not be replicated under penalty of death. Also, at some point, the Israelites brought too many resources to build the Tabernacle. Instead of paying themselves out of the surplus, they went to Moses, who resolved the problem by asking the Israelites to stop bringing gold, silver, and other offerings. He and his men put their means of living aside and worked for the Lord. This list is probably far from being thorough and complete. We don't know much about his personal life and family, but it certainly underlines why Bezalel was chosen to work for the Lord.

In response, he and those who worked with him all received the blessing from Moses after the final inspection (Exodus 39:43) and were filled with the joy of serving the Lord More importantly, the Lord Himself approved the work: "Then the cloud covered the tabernacle of meeting, and the glory of the Lord filled the tabernacle. And Moses could not enter the tabernacle of meeting, because the cloud rested above it, and the glory of the Lord filled it."

So, how does Bezalel teach us? Begin by asking yourself the following question: Does God know you by name? Does He know who you are, and are you known for those traits that make up the people the Lord uses such as honesty, dedication, and obedience? If not, start by making a change that will attract him.

Next, be stirred by the perspective and opportunities to do the work of the Lord, whether in the spotlights or the shadows.

Consider that there is no shadow before God; He sees everything we say and do.

Ask yourself the following: What talent do I have? Whatever it is, use it for the Lord and see Him multiply it. Can you write? Cook? Host? Organize? Speak? Create? Build the Kingdom! An army is not just made up of soldiers and generals. It also comprises those who build. Paul was a tentmaker, after all!

Last, be of the type of those who catch the eyes of the Lord by their faithfulness and dedication. Work to leave a legacy that will last, serve, and cover your children and their children.

WALK BY FAITH EVERY DAY

"Well done, good and faithful servant; you were faithful over a few things; I will make you ruler over many things. Enter into the joy of your Lord" (Matthew 25:21).

REFLECTION QUESTIONS

How can you use your talents to build God's Kingdom? Do you aim at excelling in what you do? Or do you remain in the average? Which one should you pursue in the work of the Lord? How? Why?

OHOLIAB

Reading: Exodus 38:23

The construction of the Tabernacle was a monumental task that imposed a great responsibility on the person willing to accomplish it. It required more than one man's expertise. While Bezalel supervised the overall project and applied his talents to specific domains, his skills were specialized and limited, and he was unable to complete all the work required on his own. To complement Bezalel's abilities and share the responsibility, the Lord appointed a second-in-command named Oholiab. Oholiab, whose name intriguingly means "father's tent," humbly accepted this function and played a pivotal role in the construction of the Lord's dwelling place. He was tasked with overseeing the making of the more delicate creations.

Oholiab, the son of Ahisamach from the tribe of Dan, was not just another skilled artisan among the Israelites. His exceptional skills and craftsmanship set him apart, catching the eye of the Lord, who specifically chose him to collaborate with Bezalel in the divine project of constructing the Tabernacle.

All his talents, bestowed upon him by the Lord, were used in the construction of the Tabernacle. It is written multiple times that he had the skills to do all the work. His specialization was more artistic. He worked with fabric. He also received the gift of teaching others in this art. Skills, especially if they come from the Lord, are not for our use only. They must be passed on, used, and taught. He was blessed to bless others. He was also skilled at teaching others: The Bible clearly states that many more men and women joined in the design and creation of the Tabernacle (Exodus 35:25–26, 36:1).

We are created in God's image and, as such, have within us the capacity to develop, design, and be artistic. Creativity was an expression of the divine in us. However, Satan diverted it from its original use for his worship[7].

Since Oholiab's talents were in fabric, he was also responsible for creating the garments of ministry for Aaron's sons, the holy garments for Aaron (Exodus 39:1), which included the ephod, shoulder straps, breastplate, tunics of fine linen, short trousers, hats, and holy crown, all after a model given by the Lord. Everything was artistically woven (Exodus 39:27) and exquisite (Exodus 39:28).

---

7   See the following chapter on Asaph.

Oholiab's responsibilities extended beyond fabric work. He was likely supervising the sewing of the tent and all the various fabrics used in its construction. These included fine linen, goat's hair, ramskins, and the art of dying fabric in blue, purple, and scarlet. His work had to be precise, as the Israelites at the time lived in the middle of the desert, leaving no room for error.

There were likely many men and women among the Israelites who were skilled in working with fabric and creating garments. However, one stood out in the eyes of the Lord because he was trustworthy and a skilled artisan. Moses himself introduced him to the Israelites in Exodus as such, so that no one could challenge his function.

Among Oholiab's notable character traits, the first is obedience. We know that obedience is vital in serving the Lord and that it draws His attention. The sentence "as the Lord commanded Moses" is repeated multiple times in the chapters describing the construction of the Tabernacle, like a chorus (Exodus 39:5–7, 21, 26, 29, 31). This was no creative license, but a work of love and obedience. Oholiab had to be able to visualize and understand the designs Moses brought to him and create them exactly as directed.

Second, Oholiab's skills complemented those of Bezalel. Both were talented in different areas, and their collaboration resulted in the construction of the Tent of the Lord. There was no time for competition, no place for ego, because they both possessed "a willing heart." Actually, the Bible says that all those who worked on the Tabernacle were "of a willing heart" (Exodus 35:5, 21–22,

26, 29, 36:2). All were working on the same project with only one thing in mind: building the tent of the Lord for His glory, not their own.

There are many lessons we can draw from Oholiab's life. Work with others toward the same goal: building the Lord's Kingdom. We are not working to build our kingdom, or an ephemeral kingdom, but an eternal one. Don't boast about your giftings or ability. These were Satan's downfall. Keep in mind that everything you have, everything you are, is from the Lord and was given to you by grace, and out of love. Do not try to excel in something that is not your area of expertise, but strive to excel in what you know. If you are faithful in small things, He will give you other responsibilities, gifts that will grow with you as you march and build the Kingdom. Do not try to do everything on your own, beyond your capabilities, or alone. The work of the Lord is a testament to the power of teamwork. We are not competing for the most significant numbers because we are not working to build our kingdom or put our name on a ministry. Everything is for the Lord. If we remember that, competition and rivalries will disappear, and we will all work "of a willing heart" for the Lord.

What talent, art, or skill do you possess that you could use to serve the Lord and build His Kingdom? These do not have to be artistic. Some are good at writing, others at hosting or organizing. Satan would like you to believe that you have nothing, but this is a lie from the pit of Hell. God invested in you and gave you a gift to use for his glory. Do not bury it, but take it out. Invest it and multiply like Oholiab did.

WALK BY FAITH EVERY DAY

"He has made the earth by His power,
He has established the world by His wisdom,
And has stretched out the heavens at His discretion"
(Jeremiah 10:12).

REFLECTION QUESTIONS

You have already considered your talents and gifts as you read about Oholiab and Bezalel. How can you collaborate with others to develop their talents and help them succeed? How can your talents contribute to building and helping others?

ASAPH

In the Bible, some of the psalms are devoted to worshiping God, expressing His grandeur and magnificence. Others are more introspective, revealing the evolution of the writer from an inner perspective, as they grapple with contradictory feelings about justice and love. Since the Levites were in charge of worship in the Tabernacle and the temple, many of the psalms were written by them; the sons of Korah, Moses, and Miriam are some of the most famous writers. A portion of the psalms published in the Old Testament was created by Asaph, a Levite himself, son of Berachiah. Many of his creations have been incorporated into modern worship songs or have at least inspired some of them.

Asaph, a Gershonite, served as a musician and singer in the Tabernacle and the temple. His role was not just that of a performer but a spiritual leader who used his talents to guide the people in worship and praise, leading them into the presence of the Lord. He played a pivotal role in the nation's spiritual life under the reigns of King David and Solomon. Asaph was gifted in many arts: He was a poet, a writer, a musician, a singer, and a composer. He wrote twelve psalms: (Psalms 50 and 73–83).

Asaph's artistic talents were not confined to personal expression or worship but also served a profound prophetic purpose. Some of his psalms directly conveyed the thoughts of the Lord, such as Psalm 50, while others served as warnings to the Israelites about their sin and behavior. His music was a powerful medium through which the Lord's messages were communicated, revealing the transformative potential of artistic expression in service to the Lord. When we use our creative gifts for God, we not only glorify Him but also inspire awe and reverence in others, drawing them closer to the divine. Asaph's example shows that creativity, when used for the Lord, can have a profound impact on those around.

He was also a religious public servant, as a Levite, whose duties were to the house of the Lord. He was gifted in multiple arts. Instead of making a secular living off of his skills, he put them to the service of the Lord, working in the temple. His gifts were notable and well-known to all; he was commissioned by King David to oversee the singing in the house of the Lord (1 Chronicles 6:16–32) and served under King Solomon's reign in the temple.

Asaph's life and work also illustrate the divine act of creation. Creativity and creation come from God: Isn't He called the

Creator? Didn't He create this universe? When the Lord created the world, as narrated in Genesis 1, He made something from Himself. He spoke, and things came to be. When He created us, He gave us the same ability as a divine gift in the form of creative skills because we are made in His image. This gift is expressed through music, the visual arts, imagination, storytelling, engineering, and many other forms of expression. Every time we create something or bring into existence something that is in our mind, regardless of its nature, we are utilizing the divine gift of creativity. That's why Satan is so present in everything artistic and creative: He hijacked the gift that was made to express the divine for his purpose.

As we mentioned earlier, Asaph holds a prophetic gift. Reading his psalms gives us access to Asaph's mind and faith, and the Lord's. We know he feared the Lord because he knew Him; he understood His heart and expressed it through poetry and songs. In the Bible, when writing expresses the heart or mind of the Lord, it is often written in the form of poetry or songs because poetry is the art of expressing the innermost thoughts. It's like a set of questions and answers that progress toward the conclusion. Many of the psalms of Asaph are prophetic because he passes down to the people the words and thoughts of the Lord, His feelings regarding specific topics. For example, in Psalm 50, the Lord is dissatisfied with the conduct of the Israelites who bring sacrifices one day but live contrary to their belief and the Lord's laws the rest of the week. His psalms discuss themes such as the Lord's justice and righteousness. Nothing remains hidden in the sight of the Lord. Every act, every motivation, and every thought is known to Him and recorded. Asaph called the people to repent through his songs, urging them to separate from the ways of the world and other surrounding civilizations.

Perhaps one of the most defining moments in Asaph's ministry was when he experienced the Presence of the Lord firsthand. Indeed, he was one of the musicians who performed at the dedication of the temple under Solomon. As such, he witnessed the cloud of smoke envelop the temple and the presence of the Lord establish itself in the building.

He worked to encourage and uplift his fellow human beings. His psalms reflect man's mind and feelings, such as not understanding when he sees the wicked prosper, causing distress and sadness at his or her own failures. However, it is essential to notice that he does not stay in that depressed state. He always turns to the Lord, enters His sanctuary and His presence through worship, and realizes that, despite all appearances, the Lord always has the last word and defends those who abide by His laws and love Him. His poetry illustrates the ways to emerge from a self-centered state of mind and gravitate toward the Lord and the hope that is in Him.

Asaph left us a legacy through his songs. His legacy is multifaceted, spanning both space and time. Space first because his sons continued his legacy, so he had a lasting influence on his family, Jerusalem, and the Israeli kingdom. As he led the worship in the temple for the dedication, the Lord descended and filled the temple with a cloud of smoke in response to the worship and Solomon's prayer. The people of Israel entered and experienced the presence of the Lord because of his (and others with him) leadership and worship. Obedience, which is a form of sacrifice, attracts the Lord.

In time, his descendants formed a guild of musicians that served Israel and Judah for centuries after him. His psalms are still, to this day, among the most popular and uplifting writings to the weary soul; they are a plea for salvation. The justice of the Lord is one of the most recurrent topics in his writings.

When considering Asaph, it is essential to understand that he was no exception. We have all received a gift, a talent (some more than others), to use for the Lord. Some are people of the written word; others are eloquent speakers. Some individuals may be organizers, while others serve as protectors, entertainers, hosts, and so on. You are not left aside; you were not made to be left behind. You have in yourself the ability to serve the Lord and work to build His Kingdom.

Although Satan wants us to believe the contrary, we can all create something: writing, music, drawing, painting, words, storytelling. The question is, what will we do with it? Will we keep it for our own sake? Will we share it with the world? Will we use it to represent the Lord and tell of His goodness and beauty? What will you do with the gifts the Lord gave you?

WALK BY FAITH EVERY DAY

"Call upon Me in the day of trouble; I will deliver you, and you shall glorify Me" (Psalm 50:15), by Asaph.

REFLECTION QUESTIONS

Which gift or talent, or ability, do you have? How do you usually use them? How can you use them for the Lord? Did Satan use this gift for his own benefit? How?

Think also about the legacy you want to leave to your children and your children's children. How can these abilities contribute to building a lasting legacy?

PART 7

Those Who Were Generous

Illustration 7: The magi

It is common to say that from the abundance of the heart the mouth speaks. I will add that from the abundance of the heart, the hand gives. Generosity is a sign of a trusting, renewed heart. Giving is part of the Christian life. If it was 10 percent in the Old Testament, it became a reflection of what we had in our hearts in the New Testament. The Bible is full of testimonies of men and women who gave without limitation or consideration. The Magi and the group of women who followed Jesus Christ in His ministry to provide for His needs and His disciples are some inspiring examples among many others.

THE MAGI

Reading: Matthew 2:1-23

Soon after Jesus' birth (within the following two years), visitors began to come to honor Him as the Savior and King. Among those visitors were men from the East, magi, who traveled a long way to celebrate the King of kings. Matthew did not reveal many details surrounding their visit; he never mentions their names, their number, or their exact origin. Still, he considered this visit significant enough to be reported in his writing.

These magi were not Jews; they were men of science from the Orient who observed the sky, probably dwelt in astrology and other pagan rituals. Used to observe the sky and the stars, they noted that nature had altered, and this change testified to a significant event, which we know was the birth of Christ on earth as a human being. These men were able to discern the signs and the times, whereas the Jews were not. The star probably shone brightly in the sky for some time (Herod's calculations cover almost two years), and no one except them came to worship. After a long journey, upon their arrival in Jerusalem, they asked for the King of the Jews, causing confusion among everyone who had remained oblivious to the signs nature had been displaying. Because of their devotion, God guided them safely to the house where Jesus dwelt with his parents.

They were also wealthy. When they traveled to see Jesus, they did not come empty-handed: They brought gold, frankincense, and myrrh. Numerous studies have been published on the meaning and symbolism of these gifts, so I will briefly address this topic here. Gold represented the kingship of Jesus Christ. It was a symbol of wealth and power, intended not as a gift for a child, but for a king. It could be used later to purchase all the necessities of life, especially during the exile in Egypt. Frankincense, a resin with healing properties, represented the divinity and priesthood of Christ. It was used in the making of the holy perfume in the temple, which no one was to imitate upon penalty of death. It was also used in offerings and burned in the sanctuary to represent the prayers of the saints. Myrrh, another type of tree resin with healing properties, was used in religious ceremonies such as burials. When Jesus was on the cross, the Roman soldiers offered him wine mixed with myrrh on a sponge to drink, which he refused to take. Myrrh likely figured among the spices used by the women the day after Jesus' burial, when they came to prepare His body. Like gold, myrrh, and frankincense could be sold and provide for future needs.

They came prepared to meet with a king and worship with what they owed that was the most precious.

At the end of the story, although they came through Jerusalem, they left another way, the Bible says. Herod had tricked these men into confiding in him, but they knew how to recognize the voice of God, and they disobeyed Herod's command to return with more information. Herod was the most powerful man in Judea at the time. This act of disobedience was not a rebellion against authority, but a demonstration of their unwavering faith and obedience to God.

These men speak to us still today. Their non-Jewish background is significant because it demonstrates God's plan to make salvation available to all people, not just the Jews. They also remind us that God speaks through signs, wonders, and dreams. Will we listen to Him? Imagine what would have happened if they had disregarded their dreams?

Herod was the most powerful man at the time, yet they did not cower before any man, no matter how powerful, but instead, they chose to obey God's command. As a result, God led them to their destination because they were determined to seek. Those who earnestly seek will find answers, and God will lead them to the ultimate truth, Jesus Christ.

Last but not least, they were lavish in their generosity. They traveled carrying gifts of great value without any consideration for the risks on their lives. They gave to the King of kings, they worshipped Him through offering of inestimable value, and they provided for the needs of the family as hard times were about to come on them.

WALK BY FAITH EVERY DAY

"Give, and it will be given to you: good measure, pressed down, shaken together, and running over will be put into your bosom. For with the same measure that you use, it will be measured back to you" (Luke 6:38).

REFLECTION QUESTIONS

God's plan for salvation is for everyone, whatever their background. How can you support the spreading of the Gospel to other nations and cultures today? Have you been attentive to the signs lately? Did you notice anything in the news, nature, or culture? How can these signs influence you in your decision-making?

JOANNA, SUSANNA, MARY MAGDALENE, AND MANY OTHERS

Reading: Luke 8:2, 3

Just as men were sent to the front during the two World Wars to fight for their country, women did not remain idle in the background. They took a stand to support the troops on the front lines, dedicating their time and energy to assist the war effort, and took on traditionally male roles in factories and other production sites. They became the driving force of the war, the fuel that powered the armies and kept the soldiers going. Although they stood behind the scenes, no fight would have been possible without the support and work of these women, and certainly no victory would have been achieved. In the spiritual realm, we find the same organization: while some are on the forefront, preaching, teaching, evangelizing, others remain in the back providing financial support, prayer support, and moral support. There is no shame in being in the back, in the shadows. Even if standing and working in the shadows, the efforts are directed toward the same aim: to win over souls and build the Kingdom of God. An army is more than just a group of soldiers standing on the frontline. It is nothing without those working behind.

When Jesus came to Earth to take on a human form, He did it thoroughly and planned to live like humans did. Jesus was hungry, thirsty, and tired. Although we know of two occasions when He fed the crowd miraculously (Matthew 14:13–21; Mark 6:30–44; Luke 9:10–17; John 6:1–14), for the rest of the time, He ate like His fellow companions. He relied on natural processes to sustain Himself: through His work as a carpenter and the generosity of others. We read about Him sitting at the table of Pharisees to dine multiple times (Luke 7:36–37, 14:1-6, 11:37, 14:1–6); we read about Him fasting (Luke 4:2); we see Him being invited to a wedding (John 2:1); or being asked at the friendly house of Martha and Mary (Luke 10:38); or we see Him dining at a publican's house named Zacchaeus (Luke 19:1–10). He had a job and trained as a carpenter, which was a good position at the time, and part of the middle class of the day. Did He continue working during His ministry? Some say yes. Others say that He stopped working as a carpenter and began working full-time at His ministry. Others say He earned some money as a carpenter and used it to provide for His needs and those of His disciples. After all, the group had a purse to hold the funds, and Judas oversaw the group's finances. If the Bible does not clearly explain His survival process, it is clear about one thing: There was a group of women "who provided for him from their substance" (Luke 8:1–3). They were Mary Magdalene, Joanna, Susana, and many others.

These women, from all social classes, made significant sacrifices in their service to Jesus. Some were married, while others were likely widowed or single. They had means of income, knew how to cook, and used their talents and goods to provide for all the needs of Jesus and His disciples for most of the duration of Jesus' earthly ministry. This includes, but is not limited to, food, clothing, and maybe even shelter. Like the disciples, the women were followers of Jesus and always stayed with Him, witnessing His teachings, the miracles, and the healings. They followed Him from village to village or town to town, bringing food or purchasing food for the group. Luke says these women had been healed from sicknesses and freed from evil spirits: Mary Magdalene had seven demons. Following their salvation, deliverance and healing, they followed Jesus out of respect for Him and thanksgiving. They were devoted to Jesus Christ.

An army is composed of soldiers, generals, and leaders. But it also includes those who, standing behind, provide for the needs of those who fight. They are as important as the soldiers because the latter would not live or fight without the providers standing behind them. They are as essential and part of victory as those on the front line. Some of us are called to be generous and provide for ministries through material possessions, donations, and sponsorship. There would be no missionary work without those who work, own businesses, contribute, pay the bills, and cover all ministry expenses. They work and give out of thankfulness and generosity. They might not be found on the front line, but they are just as much a part of the effort.

These women, known for their faithfulness, loyalty, and generosity, remained steadfast even when Jesus' disciples abandoned Him. They were standing at the foot of the cross with John. Their unwavering commitment led them to be the first to hear of the Resurrection on the third day. They were not just passive participants anymore, but active super-spreaders of the Good News. Luke 24 mentions Joanna as one of the women who continued to serve the Lord even after His death and Resurrection, actively spreading the news of His Resurrection.

Every member of the army has a unique and crucial role to play. No role should be denigrated, for in the eyes of the Lord, we are all servants of the Highest, all working to build the same Kingdom, which is not ours. Each of us, regardless of our position or resources, is integral to the mission. Our collective efforts, no matter how small they may seem, contribute to the grandeur of God's Kingdom.

Considering these women, understand that, wherever you are, you are part of a bigger effort, an army engaged in a spiritual battle against dominations and principalities. Your prayers, donations, and support all contribute to the construction, bringing a brick to the establishment of the Kingdom of God, regardless of the extent of your means. Remember these words of Jesus: "Calling his disciples to him, Jesus said, 'Truly I tell you, this poor widow has put more into the treasury than all the others. They all gave out of their wealth; but she, out of her poverty, put in everything—all she had to live on'" (Mark 12:43–44). Do not listen to the voices that say that what you do has no value, or that there is nothing you can do to help. You are called to build the Kingdom, as well as any other disciple of Jesus Christ. Do you have a gift or a talent? Use it for God! Be generous. I am an academic by trade and training, and one day I decided not only to use the skills associated with this job for academia, but also for the benefit of the Kingdom. Now, I write Christian books, screenplays, and publish other works.

No one is too small or too broken to serve in the Kingdom. When Jesus heals you and you repent from your sins, you become a new creation in Christ. Remember that Mary Magdalene had seven demons in her before she met Jesus Christ. She became a devoted and generous follower after that. You have a story to tell, a testimony to share. Start where you are and see what God can do with your offering. He fed the crowd of thousands with a few fish!

WALK BY FAITH EVERY DAY

"Therefore I say to you, her sins, which are many, are forgiven, for she loved much. But to whom little is forgiven, the same loves little" (Luke 7:47).

REFLECTION QUESTIONS

Take a moment to think about what it means to be generous. How can you demonstrate generosity today? What can you do today to engage on the path and join in the Lord's army?

PART 8

Those Who Didn't Doubt

Illustration 8: David's valiant men

Why did Moses see the Red Sea open? The Nile turning into blood? The glory of the Lord? Because he didn't doubt. Why didn't he doubt? Because he knew the Lord. His encounter with the burning bush on Mount Horeb transformed him from a man hiding from his past to one standing courageously to confront evil for his people. Trusting the Lord is a foundational stone of our walk by faith and not by sight. Like Moses, Caleb, the thirty-seven men of David, or the four men of faith, close the door to doubt and trust in the Lord. Hope and trust motivated them because they focused on a cause greater than themselves.

CALEB

Reading: Numbers 13 and 14

It can be challenging for a leader to go against the general consensus or public opinion. Concerns about reputation, maintaining a leadership position, or pride may influence a decision, causing one to vacillate between doing what is right and what appears to be best.

Caleb faced that choice.

Numbers 13:3 introduces Caleb as the son of Jephunneh and a leader of the tribe of Judah. As such, he was a public figure among the Hebrews. He was known, trusted, and respected since he was handpicked by Moses himself, following the Lord's direct order, to be one of the twelve spies sent to explore the Promised Land. These men were tasked with exploring and reporting on the people, the land, the cities, and other aspects of the region. Decisions and conquest strategies would then be based on the report of these twelve spies.

Upon their return, and after forty days of careful exploration, the twelve spies submitted their report. It was not all that great. Fear took over the thoughts and hearts of ten of the spies, leading to a refusal to enter and conquer the Promised Land despite the Lord's commands. It was at that moment that Caleb's situation began to turn sour as he publicly disagreed with the other spies, and he found himself alone against ten other men regarding the strategic approach to conquest. Although ten spies argued that it was impossible to take the land, Caleb and later Joshua chose to believe it was possible. Soon afterward, the Hebrews, contaminated by the views of the other ten spies, threatened to stone Caleb and Joshua.

Caleb did not conform to the status quo. He became a dissident voice—something that those who follow Christ and God's principles often experience. How did he stand out and make a difference?

First, the ten spies based their argument on a false assumption: In verse 27, they said to Moses, "The land where YOU sent us" (emphasis mine). Their first mistake was to associate Moses with the idea of entering the Promised Land. It was clear in verse 2 that the idea came from a direct command from the Lord. Instead of remembering that the Lord was with them, their perspective switched to man and his limitations. Because they failed to concentrate on the Lord, they forgot all the miracles and signs He had already performed. Caleb's perspective, on the other hand, remained focused on the Lord: "Only do not rebel against the Lord, nor fear the people of the land, for they are our bread; their protection has departed from them, and the Lord is with us. Do not fear them," he said (Numbers 14:9).

Second, the ten spies let appearances cloud their judgment and decision-making process. They admitted that the land was as described: "It truly flows with milk and honey, and this is its fruit" (Numbers 13:27). But right after, they went on to the negatives: The people were strong, the cities fortified and large, and there were descendants of Anak, Hittites, Jebusites, Amorites, and Canaanites. The ten spies were cultivating their anxieties through negative thoughts and feeding them to the Hebrews. They relied on what they saw. Caleb saw the same thing; however, in verse 30, he stood out: Yes, there were big people, a lot of them, but these were appearances, and they could be defeated because God was with them.

Third, as you observe how the Hebrews fed these growing anxiety monsters that settle more deeply in their minds and hearts, all the Israelites joined in the defeated mindset, repeating over and over the same message: "That night, all the members of the community raised their voices and wept aloud. All the Israelites grumbled against Moses and Aaron, and the whole assembly said to them, 'If only we had died in Egypt! Or in this wilderness! Why is the Lord bringing us to this land only to let us fall by the sword? Our wives and children will be taken as plunder. Wouldn't it be better for us to go back to Egypt?' And they said to each other, 'We should choose a leader and go back to Egypt'" (Numbers 14:1–4). These thoughts spread through the population, being passed from person to person, infecting minds like an epidemic. However, as the spies spread negativity, Caleb did not let doubt, fear, or anxiety take control of his mind (Numbers 13:30). It is written that he silenced the ten men (Numbers 13:30), opposing them with these words: "Let us go up at once and take possession, for we are well able to overcome it." He added later, "If the Lord delights in us, then He will bring us into this land and give it to us" (Numbers 14:8). 2 Corinthians 5:7 says that the followers of Christ "walk by faith and not by sight." They do not depend on what surrounds them or what is visible to them.

Fourth, the Lord never said it would be easy. The Hebrews had to conquer the Promised Land through force and warfare. Going back in time, He initially gave everything to Adam and Eve, and we know what they did with it. When they fell, they switched allegiance and handed over to Satan what the Lord had entrusted to them. All authority over Creation was transferred from Adam and Eve to Satan. Logically, Satan appointed his human agents to manage the Creation: The Hittites, the Canaanites, and others. Caleb understood the realities of the conquest war. His words reflected those of a warlord rallying his troops. As he stood alone at first, then with Joshua, things started to get very heated. Moses and Aaron fell to their faces, and the Hebrews said, "to stone them with stones" (Numbers 14:10). Death felt very real. But the story does not end there. While the people were picking up stones, "the glory of the Lord appeared in the tabernacle of meeting before the children of Israel" (Numbers 14:10). So, when the time came, the Lord took their side and defended them against all their opponents: the ten spies died of a plague.

What can we learn from Caleb's story? I see seven lessons we can draw from the testimony of Caleb and Joshua's faith. However, I am sure there are more!

As a leader, we must always seek what is in the best interest and what is right for the people under our responsibility. As Caleb, point them toward God, be the light, the salt, a role model that speaks in words and actions. Words can lie, but actions cannot.

Base every decision and your values on the Lord. Would this be offensive to Him? Could it have repercussions for me and my family? What type? It is important not to walk by sight but by faith. God is the immovable rock that will sustain life's tempests, earthquakes, and hurricanes.

Silence the voices that cause you to be anxious and worried. They are like monsters that feed each other and eat you alive from the inside. Do not invite them in, but nourish your soul with the promises of the Lord. When your natural eyes scare you, use your spiritual eyes and look up to the Lord. A man or a woman who loses sight of God is limited in his or her capacities. God is eternal, almighty, and powerful. Silence the voices that kill your dreams, your projects, like Caleb did.

Choose God even when the perspective of conflict or death arises. He will show up and fight your battles. You will become the spectator of the defeat and demise of your enemies. Indeed, God pronounced a death sentence on all those who did not trust Him (Numbers 14: 24), and Caleb and Joshua received the promise that they would enter and possess the land. Something not even Moses and Aaron were granted.

Do not be afraid, even when alone against the world, for God will show up. Romans 8:31 says: "If God is for us, who can stand against us?" Caleb's courage and determination attracted the Lord's attention because he had "a different spirit in him and has followed me fully," says the Lord (Numbers 14:24). None of your actions and decisions fall into oblivion. The Lord knows and remembers them all.

In Numbers 14:37, the ten spies died by a plague before the Lord. Doubt, fear, and anxiety will kill you and your faith if you allow them to come in, and it will spread to the others around you. Do not feed or listen to them.

Lastly, leave a legacy that will mark and bless the generations after you. Caleb was a member of the tribe of Judah, the tribe that, along with Benjamin, formed the future Kingdom of Judah after the division of Israel. Caleb waited forty years to take possession of his land. He was well over eighty years old when the promise became reality. The important thing is that he received it. Learn from him, do not fear, choose God, and He will show up for you at the right time, and the generations after you will be blessed. Claim and take possession of the promises you received. Walking with God is a lifelong process.

WALK BY FAITH EVERY DAY

"Walk by faith and not by sight" (2 Corinthians 5:7).

REFLECTION QUESTIONS

Think of a time when you took God's side, like Caleb, and went against the general consensus. What were the circumstances? Was it difficult? Why or why not? Why did you decide to make that decision? How can you take God's side today?

THE THIRTY-SEVEN MIGHTY MEN OF KING DAVID

Reading: 2 Samuel 23:8–39

Lists of names and genealogies are probably some of the most challenging parts of the Bible to read. More than once, I wondered why the various authors of the Bible included these lists. Still, the Lord found it necessary to include them. If you approach the Bible with the mindset that everything in it has value and serves the purpose of teaching us, then these inventories suddenly take on new meaning. 2 Samuel 23:8–39 is one of these passages that accumulates people and place names. However, it is worthwhile to spend time considering those long, tongue-twisting lists and learn the lessons they offer us today.

It is usually understood and believed that great men throughout history did not accomplish exploits and achievements alone.

Indeed, the lone hero is a rare phenomenon, mainly found in modern comic books. There is more power, efficiency, and courage in teamwork than in solo work. King David was no exception to the rule. The Bible says in 2 Samuel 23:8–39 that David was surrounded by mighty men who accomplished exploits that constitute the stuff of legends. They were thirty-seven soldiers without whom King David's reign would have been different. They were a group of soldiers who served under the king's command and fought for him, for his fame, and their country. Just as these men served David, we too are called to serve our King, Jesus Christ, and fight for His Kingdom. Their example of courage and loyalty can inspire us in our own spiritual battles.

The Hall of Fame of the Mighty Soldiers found its place right after the last words of King David. These soldiers distinguished themselves in combat under the king's command. They are listed in descending order of strength and deeds. King David and the people of Israel knew these men very well, and they found them worthy of publicly stating their names and village of origin for future generations. They had built a reputation of courage and valor. When these men stepped on the battlefield, the opposing army knew King David meant business. Their reputation surrounded them and preceded them, and the Lord found them worthy of being remembered for these qualities. Just like King David knew these men by name, the Lord knows you by your name. However, if the king knew them, it was because of their acts and courage. Consider this: The Lord also has His eyes on you, and He watches you when you are on the battlefield, taking a stand for Him and demonstrating courage in the face of difficulties. Also, if the Lord knows your names and deeds, the demons, too, know the mighty people of God: Didn't the demons tell the seven sons of Sceva they didn't know them when they knew Jesus and Paul? See Acts 19:15: "And the evil spirit answered and said, 'Jesus I know, and Paul I know; but who are you?" That question in itself is not just scary; it is also a dire warning whether we present a threat to Satan and his servants or not, and that we build a reputation in the spiritual spheres as well as in the natural sphere.

Listing the names is a form of honor and remembrance, the same way we list the names of the soldiers who died fighting for their country on memorials: Epitaphs such as "We don't know them, but we owe them all" or "Never forget, but ever honor" or "In remembrance of the braves" often highlight the value and the price they paid for us. There is a duty of memory because these men bring upon us a responsibility to continue the work they began and protect their legacy to pass it on. Should we waste the blood they shed? Or the tears their families wept? Should we trample on their graves? These men inspire us to do more incredible things for our King. They made us feel small but not inadequate because they were men like us. The differences dwelled in an intrinsic motivation to fight for freedom, a sacred fear of God, and a sense of duty and loyalty toward the king and country. James wrote, "Elijah was a man with a nature like ours, and he prayed earnestly that it would not rain, and it did not rain on the land for three years and six months" (James 5:17).

They are here to encourage us to continue the fight and remind us that we do not fight alone. In the list, it is mentioned twice that they worked in groups of three (2 Samuel 9, 13, 18, and 22). We are a part of a bigger army composed of humans and celestial beings, led by the Lord. We do not fight alone.

To consider what it means to be called mighty in the Kingdom of God, let's look at other biblical people who receive the title of "mighty." Isaiah 6:9 says that Mighty is one of the names of Jesus Christ: "For to us a child is born, to us a son is given, and the government will be on his shoulders. And he will be called Wonderful Counselor, *Mighty God*, Everlasting Father, Prince of Peace." In Hebrew, the name is *El Gibbor*. So, in the Kingdom of God, a mighty person is a person who wears the attributes and the name of Christ.

In addition, we all recall that in Judges 6, the Angel of the Lord calls Gideon a "mighty man of valor" when he certainly did not feel that way, was plagued with fear, and was hiding. Gideon was not born with might and courage. He acquired these traits as he walked through the following weeks with the Lord in obedience and respect, taking one step at a time, starting with small actions, which grew bigger and bigger every time he obeyed. The closer he was to the Lord, the more he built might and courage in his heart. Might and valor come from the Lord and are built over time and experience. Nimrod, in Genesis 10:8–12, is called a mighty man before the Lord, a mighty hunter, and Jephthah, the judge, was another man to receive the qualification of mighty. A person of might and valor is certainly not reckless nor imprudent. It's a trait that, like courage, guides a person's actions and seeks the Lord's advice. It is built through time and experience. The more we walk close to the Lord, the more we understand His character, the more He dwells in us, and the more we reflect His traits.

They were men with the same limitations and capacities as any other man on planet Earth. They were all human, made of flesh and bones like us. None of these men was born with might and valor. They started as babies on their mother's lap. They grew and built character traits by hearing the stories of great men, training, learning, and in the knowledge of the Lord. They received this attribute because of their actions and the decisions they made when facing danger. Nelson Mandela, the first Black president of South Africa, famously said that "courage was not the absence of fear, but the triumph over it." Courage is like a muscle; you build it by making tough, unpopular decisions and facing your fears on the spiritual battlefield. Your reputation, whatever it is, will precede you in the natural and the spiritual spheres. Your deeds and courage will be an example for others to follow in your footsteps and make a difference. Paul wrote to the Philippians: "the things which happened to me have actually turned out for the furtherance of the gospel, so that it has become evident to the whole palace guard, and to all the rest, that my chains are in Christ; and most of the brethren in the Lord, having become confident by my chains, are much more bold to speak the word without fear" (Philippians 1:12–14).

Might and valor were the attributes of all thirty-seven men, although they are presented in descending order, the mightiest first, etc. There is a gradation in might. However, the essential components might remain the same from the least to the most. Each one of these soldiers was famous for something particular. Let's see some examples:

- Josheb-Basshebeth the Tachmonite received the nickname of Adino the Eznite because he "lifted his spear against eight hundred, whom he slew at one time" (2 Samuel 23:8). He finished the work. He was strong in combat: How does one become strong? By training, practicing, hanging around like-minded people, and participating in the heat of the battle.
- Eleazar, the son of Dodo, did not let circumstances dictate his response. Still, his knowledge of the truth guided his actions (2 Samuel 23:8) despite being tired or wounded: "He arose and smote the Philistines until his hand was weary, and his hand clave unto the sword."
- Shammah, the son of Agee the Hararite, remained loyal to the king in the face of danger (2 Samuel 23:9). When everyone else fled the scene of the battle (2 Samuel 23:11–12), he stayed and fought for what was right, whatever the size or value: He defended a field of lentils.
- They risked their lives to answer their king's wish, entering the Philistines' encampment by night to find water for David from the well of Bethlehem (2 Samuel 23:13–17).
- Benaiah, the son of Jehoiada, himself the son of a brave man, knew the one with him was greater than the one against him. He did not fear nature and fought lions when necessary (2 Samuel 23:21), chasing them

down to their lair. He did not look at appearances and fought like a lion against the Moabites and an Egyptian and won.

They were all devoted to their king (2 Samuel 23:13–17), Israel, and the Lord, the kingdom to which they belonged, and fought for what was more important than their lives and well-being. Uriah the Hittite, the last of the list (2 Samuel 23:39), came back from battle when called by the king. Despite the king's orders, he refuses to go to his house and sleeps in his bed because his companions of arms are fighting on the battlefield; the story of David, Bath-Sheba, and Uriah shows that they were even loyal to a fault:

> But Uriah slept at the door of the king's house with all the servants of his Lord and did not go down to his house. So when they told David, "Uriah did not go down to his house," David said to Uriah, "Did you not come from a journey? Why did you not go down to your house?" And Uriah said to David, "The ark and Israel and Judah are dwelling in tents, and my Lord Joab and the servants of my Lord are encamped in the open fields. Shall I then go to my house to eat, drink, and lie with my wife? I will not do this thing as you live and as your soul lives."

More importantly, each of them knew who they were fighting for and why, and understood the risks involved in the process. Their eyes were fixed on the prize, as Paul wrote in Philippians

3:13–14: "Brothers, I do not consider that I have made it my own. But one thing I do: forgetting what lies behind and straining forward to what lies ahead, I press on toward the goal for the prize of the upward call of God in Christ Jesus."

They cast away the lions and the giants of their lives. They didn't look at appearances; they did not allow fear to dwell in their hearts because they knew the one fighting with them was greater than the one standing against them. Like these men, live a life worthy of remembering. Live a life that will make a difference. Be remembered for your love, your encouragements, and be worthy of these words of Jesus: "Well done, good and faithful servant; you were faithful over a few things, I will make you ruler over many things. Enter into the joy of your Lord" (Matthew 25:21). We are not all called to accomplish the same things. We are not all called to serve on the mission field. We are not all called to stand under the spotlights on a stage. Most of us will pass unnoticed to the average Christian. Most of our actions will remain unknown to our pastors. However, we are all called to serve. And, as King David knew his valorous men, the Lord, our King, knows His soldiers. If you consider this, you will never fight in spiritual battles the same; you will never feel alone again.

Because of this, the Lord used them to bring great victory to Israel (2 Samuel 23:10 and 12).

In conclusion, these men had one thing in mind: to serve. They foreshadowed the words of Apostle Paul to the Colossians 3:23: "And whatever you do, do it heartily, as to the Lord and not to men." We, too, should become men and women of courage, mighty in the Kingdom, fighting under the eyes of our Lord, even if it means we will never receive rewards on this planet.

What motivated these men was that they knew why they were fighting. Their motivation came from within themselves and the teachings they received. Today, would we be called mighty men and women of God? Display courage and strength, not as the world defines them but as the Lord does. A mighty man, a mighty woman, is still human. The difference resides in what lies behind appearances. Will our circumstances define our identity, or will the unshakable knowledge that we are part of a greater army guide us in our decisions?

WALK BY FAITH EVERY DAY

"Not that I have already attained, or am already perfected; but I press on, that I may lay hold of that for which Christ Jesus has also laid hold of me. Brethren, I do not count myself to have apprehended; but one thing I do, forgetting those things which are behind and reaching forward to those things which are ahead, I press toward the goal for the prize of the upward call of God in Christ Jesus" (Philippians 3:12–14).

REFLECTION QUESTIONS

What does it mean to be a valiant hero for the Lord today?

How can the idea that you are part of a greater army influence you to make a decision?

David had thirty-seven men to help him. How can you help someone today to win for the Lord and become a valiant hero (change their perception of themselves)?

154

THE FOUR MEN OF RELENTLESS FAITH

Reading: Mark 2:3–5 and Luke 5:18–25

After being rejected in His hometown of Nazareth, Jesus relocated to Capernaum, where He established His Galilean ministry headquarters. In those days, Capernaum was an important town because it was strategically located on the northwestern shore of the Sea of Galilee at the crossroads of trade routes. It housed a Roman garrison, a bustling fishing community, and was a popular stop for many travelers and tradespeople. As such, it was quite populated and bustling. It was easy to get lost in such a crowded city, to pass unnoticed, or to be forgotten—especially for certain groups like widows, orphans, and the sick. Mark 2:3–5 and Luke 5:18–25 tell the story of a member of one of these marginalized groups—a paralyzed man—and how his encounter with Jesus Christ changed his life.

In ancient times, being paralyzed often signified the end of a meaningful life. Paralyzed people usually relied on family or friends for food, basic needs, and care. However, Capernaum also counted among its inhabitants a group of four men of relentless faith who moved mountains—or, in this case, uncovered a house—to see their paralyzed friend's life changed. These are the men I will call the Four Men Relentless of Faith.

This is how the story goes. One day, Jesus was teaching in a house in Capernaum. As usual, His fame drew many—some to see Him, others to hear Him. Mark and Luke write that among the crowd were locals, people from neighboring villages, and others who came all the way from Jerusalem. It also included village dwellers, scribes, Pharisees, and teachers of the Law. Knowing Jesus was in town, four men decided to bring a paralyzed man to Him for healing. We don't know anything about these four men aside from their faith. What were their names? Social status? Origin? Mark and Luke don't mention this information. But these men were driven by an unyielding desire to see their friend's (or brother's or father's) life changed. So, they picked up the man and his bed and walked to the house where Jesus was. When they arrived, a crowd stood in front of the door, blocking the way—a crowd that remained blind to the needs of the paralyzed. The four men did not give up. Seeing the fifth man on his bed, they decided to do the unthinkable: Since they could not storm the door, they stormed the roof. They removed, one by one, the tiles of the roof that blocked the way to Jesus. Once the roof was open, they lowered the man on his bed to the feet of Jesus amidst the crowd (Luke 5:20). And the rest is history: Jesus forgave the paralyzed man's sins, and he was restored to health, walking away from a crowd in shock, carrying his bed.

Imagine, for an instant, the reunion between this man and his friends outside the house! The once-paralyzed man, who was carried on a bed to Jesus, now walks back home, holding his bed. This transformation, from a state of helplessness to one of independence, is a powerful testament to the miraculous power of Jesus.

There are many valuable lessons to learn from this testimony. The first lesson is that if you invite Jesus into your house, your life, or your heart, things will change. You and your home will never be the same. People will be drawn to you (for better or worse). When Jesus enters your house, He will lift the roof of human limitations; miracles, divine power, and deliverance will happen. He moves beyond our human sphere, and so will you.

Second, if you want to witness a miracle, you need to know where to go. The four men knew where Jesus was, and they walked straight to Him. They did not run around in circles looking for a human solution or a temporary fix to their problem. They walked straight to Jesus and accepted no imitation. Don't limit yourself to human possibilities, but go to Jesus. He is the direct liaison with God and the intercessor, our advocate before the Father.

Third, on your way to Jesus, just like the four men, you will encounter crowds blocking the way. Pharisees, scribes, and teachers of the Law will be among the crowd: Religion will try to stop you from reaching the truth; rules will bind and limit your actions; knowledge can confuse you or discourage you. If you want to get Jesus Christ, you must look beyond the crowd and block out the voices of the well-thinking people who will try to hold you back from your miracle. Don't be afraid or overwhelmed by the crowd. Tune out the voices of doubters, mockers, and despair. Find another way if you have to—go around or go above—but go to Jesus!

Once the four men reached the roof, they removed the tiles. Before approaching Jesus Christ and witnessing a miracle in your life, remove the tiles of doubt, fear, and unbelief, as well as social conventions dictated by those who think they know better, and say they always "have your best interest in mind." The four men dug a hole and cleared the way because "the power of the Lord was present for Him (Jesus) to perform healing" (Luke 5:17). They knew something would happen. The power was there, within reach. It remains here today: We still need to extend our hand and touch Jesus, bring our burdens to His feet, just as the four men did for their friend. Their faith knew no limits, yielded to no compromise, and accepted no stumbling block. As a result, their faith was rewarded. They were four men of faith who were relentless, unstoppable, unyielding, and persistent, never giving up until the Lord answered their prayer.

In conclusion, to witness miracles and salvation, storm the roof with prayers for your friends and family who are lost, sick, or discouraged. Do everything in your power to bring them to Jesus Christ.

Believe when others don't, believe when everything seems lost; believe for those who don't, who have lost faith. You will move mountains; you will walk on water. Show your faith through your actions and initiative. Don't be a faith-in-words-only person. Be proactive, and let your faith guide every step you take. This is the key to a fulfilling and transformative spiritual life.

Do not be discouraged by the surrounding crowds that may stop you from working for God and reaching your miracle. Don't let appearance and walls stop you either. Don't fight alone; don't carry your burdens by yourself. Bring them to Jesus, pray with others, and work hand in hand with the Holy Spirit. There was no competition among the four men. All were inspired by the same Spirit, working toward the same goal.

Remove the stones, the tiles that stand in your way; unforgiveness, doubt, and unbelief do not belong here! Bring your problems to the feet of Jesus, not someone else. Speak to Him first. Do not accept imitations or placeholders.

Be relentless, run the race until the end. Jesus will reward your faith, and you will please God. A miracle is within reach.

Go beyond what the masses do.

WALK BY FAITH EVERY DAY

"Now faith is confidence in what we hope for and assurance about what we do not see. This is what the ancients were commended for. By faith we understand that the universe was formed at God's command, so that what is seen was not made out of what was visible" (Hebrews 11:1–3).

REFLECTION QUESTIONS

These four men believed Jesus could heal their friend. They went above and beyond to bring him to Jesus, so that he might be healed. How can you help someone who is struggling (in life, in their faith) today? What steps can you take today to increase your faith (and others') and come out of your comfort zone? What stones do you think you should remove from your life to grow in faith?

PART 9
Those Who Were Wise

Illustration 9: Abigail and King David

Wisdom is listed in 1 Corinthians 12:8–10 as one of the nine gifts of the Spirit; however, we don't usually consider it as important as the others. It isn't often discussed from the pulpit, yet it's listed first in 1 Corinthians 12:8–10. There are several examples of men and women who exercised wisdom in the Bible. King Solomon comes to mind. However, he was not the only one. James talks about divine wisdom in his epistle, and Abraham's servant, Deborah, Abigail, and an anonymous woman from the town of Abel of Beth Maachah are all examples that inspire us to seek this wonderful gift of the Spirit.

ABRAHAM'S SERVANT

Reading: Genesis 24

Out of all the people in the Bible, if I were to choose one person to take with me on a journey, I would pick the one who showed wisdom and faithfulness: Abraham's servant. What was his name, again? Well, that is the thing. No one knows. He is a notable yet anonymous individual who remained in service throughout his life. His faithfulness, excellence, and wisdom put him under the spotlight to accomplish one of the most critical missions in the history of Israel: to find a wife for Abraham's son, Isaac, the one who would be later called Israel. He was tasked to find the woman who would give birth to the people of the Lord.

We know almost nothing about this man. Genesis 24:2 tells us he was the "eldest servant of his (Abraham's) house." And that's it. Still, the text reveals a lot about his personality, and, to be honest, isn't that what matters the most? Future generations will not remember our lives, the places we visited, or the vacations we took. Ultimately, what remains in collective memory is how we treat people, our integrity, character, and actions.

Very few anonymous people succeeded in their enterprise like this man. Alternatively, if they did, they only remained anonymous briefly. So, how was he? And what did he do to make a difference? What were the traits noted in the text that made all the difference? May they inspire us to be the same because these are common to all the people God can use.

First, we know that he was a man who could be trusted. At the time of the events narrated in Genesis 24, Abraham was an old, widowed, nearly blind, wealthy, and influential man. This servant managed all his belongings and his house. Still, he never tried to steal the riches of his master, even though the latter was unable to see. We know that he chose a reasonable number of presents to bring with him to Mesopotamia. If this man were to select the wrong woman, the future of God's people would be challenged. There would be no Israel today.

He was a man of readiness. After receiving the mission, the servant prepared carefully, anticipating all eventualities. He swore to do everything and follow all recommendations to succeed. It is written that he had at his disposal "all the goods of his master" (Genesis 24:10). Still, he took just what was necessary: camels (Genesis 24:10), "jewels of silver, and jewels of gold, and raiment" (Genesis 24:53) to give to the fiancée, and other "precious things" to give to the family, like a dowry (Genesis 24:53).

He was also a man of courage. We read this chapter in one setting in less than five minutes. In reality, the project's ensemble spans over a month and requires the engagement of many people to face numerous dangers. At the time, Abraham probably lived in Hebron, in the land of Canaan, and his family lived in Nahor. The distance between the two cities is 468 miles and would take seventeen days to walk. The dangers involved in such a journey were real. At the time of Abraham, roads were not protected by the army, unlike in Nehemiah's day. No signposts indicated the way, only the sun and the stars. There was probably no road, just a dirty path: Thieves, attacks, temptations, lousy weather, internal treason, and personal interest paved the way to Nahor. This man took great risks to carry out his master's will.

He was a man of prayer. We mentioned earlier that he was the eldest in Abraham's household. He was probably around when Sodom and Gomorrah were destroyed. He was probably around when Abraham went to save Lot. Maybe he was a young servant who fought in this battle. He grew old in the shadows of Abraham and his faith. As such, he became a man of prayer who knew the Lord. Like Abraham, he remitted his projects before the Lord and asked for a sign to guide him in his choice once he arrived at his destination. This sign follows a particular order. In his prayer, the servant sets his situation in time and space. His prayer is not vague; it is made for that moment, that mission, those circumstances. He is engaged in body and mind. Moreover, he draws in detail the expected answer, like Gideon, except that one sign was sufficient for him (but this is a whole other sermon). He asks for a sign in words and action.

He was a man of faith. The answer of the Lord was not long in coming, "And before I had done speaking in mine heart, behold, Rebekah came forth…" (Genesis 24:45). The Lord answered his prayer. However, while waiting for an answer to his prayer, the servant did not stay passive. When the girl arrived with a pitcher, he "ran to meet her" and said the exact words he had prayed. He acted, but he ran toward the prize (as Paul did).

Last, he kept his word. The servant came back with Rebekah, and the rest is history. He disappears after chapter 24 and remains living under Abraham's tent, maybe even Isaac's, happy that he accomplished what he was asked.

Like Abraham's servant, you are an ambassador. Have faith and walk like a soldier of the Lord of Hosts. Abraham's servant gathers all the qualities of an ambassador. He was sent to another country to represent his master and establish a covenant. If Abraham were to be ill-represented or his servants misbehaved, no one would have accepted joining this family in marriage, and the journey would be in vain. Before the Lord, we are responsible for carrying the Lord's promises and representing Him, His good name, and His message.

Pray for every matter of life: Pray for a spouse, for children, for a job. The Lord delights in intervening on our behalf in everyday life issues. He is a Father and wants to see His children grow. The Laws given in Deuteronomy and Leviticus are accompanied by all types of blessings that cover all aspects of personal life for those who abide by His will.

Ask for signs and wonders when unsure. The servant certainly did. Seek God's advice; pursue wisdom. You will avoid many pitfalls and traps. Wisdom is a gift of the Spirit. It is actually listed first, before all the others. It is not the most glamorous, but it is undoubtedly the most helpful for decision-making and life.

Be a person of your word. Don't make promises you are not sure to keep. May your yes be yes, and your no be no. You will build a reputation of trust and gain access to confidences. Similarly, don't spill the beans! What secret is yours to tell? None! Until he received confirmation that he was on the right track and that Rebekah was the right woman for Isaac, he said nothing about his journey.

The servant won his master's trust to the point that Abraham entrusted him with the management of all he owned and the future of his only son, the son of the promise the Lord had made to Abraham. No man will be more celebrated or known for his obedience than he. He received an entire (modern) chapter in the book of Genesis.

WALK BY FAITH EVERY DAY

"The fear of the Lord is the beginning of wisdom,
And the knowledge of the Holy One is understanding"
(Proverbs 9:10).

REFLECTION QUESTIONS

How did the servant demonstrate wisdom and trustworthiness during his mission?

Trust is a fragile bond between people; yet, it is the foundation of all relationships on this planet. It is what reputation, marriage, contracts, and business are built on. Are you trustworthy? How do you show this character trait in your everyday life and to the people around you? Or if you lack in this domain, what can you do today to grow in this?

DEBORAH

Reading: Judges 4 and 5

Decisions affect everything. So does indecision, disobedience, and fear. If you don't do what you are called to do, if you don't accomplish the mission the Lord has in store for you, He will find someone else to do it. Walking with God is a journey in faith, not sight. Deborah rose because Barak refused to obey the Lord. Because of his hesitation and fears, even if he eventually completed the work he was instructed to do, he received no glory. This is a stark reminder of the consequences of disobedience and the importance of obedience in fulfilling God's plan.

Going back in time, just before the conquest, Joshua had reproached some of the tribes for not completing the conquest and choosing to live in compromise with the Canaanites (Joshua 23:4–5). At the time Deborah became the fourth judge in Israel, the Hebrews had been living under the Canaanites' oppression because of their sins and their delay in obeying the Lord's commands to conquer the Promised Land (which includes to cast away its former inhabitants: the Canaanites, Midianites, etc.).

This oppression came to be because soon after Ehud died (he was the third judge who had delivered the Hebrews from the oppression of the Midianites), they walked away from the Lord's Laws, adopting local religions and rituals. So, another twenty years of harsh oppression began for the children of Israel. They adopted the rites and beliefs of their neighbors, the Canaanites, who then entered the land, stole the crops, and destroyed everything by means of incursions and persecution. Leviticus 26 explains that if the Israelites were disobedient, the Lord would bring a nation to steal the harvest, destroy the cities, and inflict other punishments. The Israelites were facing the consequences of their disobedience and rebellion for which they had been warned.

Amid their troubles, the children of Israel remembered that they had a God, and they cried to Him. He found a woman to answer the call and deliver them. Her name was Deborah. Deborah was living a fairly ordinary life. She was married to a man named Lapidoth. Deborah was also a prophetess. She could hear the Lord and share His Word to those around her. She had a spot under a tree where everyone knew she would dispense judgment, and it was a place where they could seek advice, fairness, and justice. She answered a calling when no one else did. She became the fourth judge in Israel since the death of Joshua, and the only woman to fulfill the duties of a judge.

There were only twelve judges total between the death of Joshua and the crowning of Saul as King of Israel. Her duties were to rule over the people. She was a military commander and a leader with civil authority. In Judges 6:4, Deborah sends for Barak, the son of Abinoam from Kedesh, in Naphthali. Once he is in her presence, she reveals out loud what the Lord had commanded Barak: to go and set Israel free from the oppression of the Canaanites: "Has not the Lord God of Israel commanded…" she says. This affirmation is troubling because Barak was aware of his calling in life, but he refused to obey. Was it because he did not trust the Lord, or was he scared? Did he perceive his responsibilities toward his family as too important to risk everything in leading the Israelite army? This is to say that even after the Lord spoke publicly to Barak through the voice of Deborah, Barak still refused to go unless Deborah went with him. He feared the Canaanites more than the Lord. Still, the Lord did not just call Barak to action; He gave him a complete strategy to follow in verse 6: "Go and deploy troops at Mount Tabor; take with you ten thousand men of the sons of Naphtali and of the sons of Zebulun; and against you I will deploy Sisera, the commander of Jabin's army, with his chariots and his multitude at the River Kishon." The Lord gave every detail, up to the number of men and tribes they came from. Moreover, the strategy came with a promise: "…and I will deliver him (Sisera) into your hand" (Judges 4:7). Even after all this and Deborah's intervention, Barak still did not fully trust the Lord. He needed an anchor to cling to, walking by sight rather than by faith. He had to see the presence of the Lord through Deborah to go confidently. This lack of trust and his unwillingness to obey robbed him of reaping the glory of victory. All the glory was given to another obscure woman named Jael. This serves as a reminder of the importance of trust in God's plan, even when it seems uncertain.

Deborah's faith in the Lord and His promises was unwavering. She never mocked or scoffed at Barak, but instead, her faith encouraged him to lead the armies to battle and win. Her trust in the Lord's plan, even when it wasn't her role or duty, is a powerful example of faith in action. So, after Deborah said she would march with him, Barak decided to go and hire the men of the two tribes. He placed the ten thousand men on Mount Tabor, just like the Lord ordered. However, as he moves in faith, Satan also moves his pawns: the descendants of Moses' father-in-law, who had settled not too far away, ran to Sisera and betrayed Barak, providing information on his moves and strategies.

Then came the battle.

As Barak faced Sisera, Deborah released a war cry over the Israelites, claiming the promise made to Barak for that day: "Up! For this is the day in which the Lord has delivered Sisera into your hand. Has not the Lord gone out before you?" (Judges 4:14). She proclaimed that the Lord was already on the battlefield and fighting for His children. Following this release, Sisera fled with all his men and chariots. So, Barak and his men showed up and finished the work; they annihilated Sisera's army.

So, what can we learn from Deborah and Barak?

First, by not completing the conquest and leaving some of the Canaanites and Midianites, among others, to remain in the land, they became a thorn in the side of the Hebrews and a stumbling block. If you live the life of a disciple of Jesus Christ and do not sever ties with your old life, you will have a hard time, because the fight between good and evil will be raging inside you. Sever all ties with sin, old temptations. Do not even look at them, do not allow them to come close to you, do not open the door to them, or, they will become a thorn in your flesh, keeping you defeated and in a perpetual struggle when the Lord gave you the power to resist and be free!

Second, the Israelites were guilty of idolatry, among other things. They copied the lifestyle of the Canaanites. If you copy the world, the spirit of the world will enter your life, steal your joy, cut your resources, and destroy everything you built with the Lord because you opened a door. Remember what God told Cain: "…sin lies at the door. And its desire is for you, but you should rule over it" (Genesis 4:7).

Third, God seeks ordinary people like Deborah to accomplish extraordinary acts. People who will obey him. That could be you, if you are willing to.

Next, you need a "tree of Deborah," a place where you go to seek the Lord's presence. Everyone knew where the tree was; your behavior and wisdom should be known to others so that they may come to you to seek advice and grow spiritually, becoming spiritual leaders in their own right. Your spiritual power coming from above will be known to all, and they will come to you.

Fourth, we see that God had a plan to deliver Israel through the hand and leadership of Barak. However, his disobedience kept Israel in bondage longer than necessary and delayed God's plan and Israel's freedom. Fear the Lord more than men. Your disobedience can delay God's plan and the salvation of those around you, prolonging their misery when you hold the key to their solution. Is this really what you want? Understand that the Lord will not send you without a plan or support. As in military warfare, strategies and tactics pave the roads to victory. The Holy Spirit will walk with you, and the Lord will direct your steps.

Next, to receive the promises, obey God, follow His plan, and trust Him. Have faith. When God asks you something, He will go with you, and He will give you the necessary steps to succeed. Among His many names is the Lord of Hosts, or armies. All Barak had to do to see his people free was to trust and obey. Walk by faith, not by sight (Paul and Thomas). Fear, doubt, and disobedience will prevent you from reaping the prize the Lord has reserved for you. If you don't do, or delay, what the Lord has asked you to do, He might take it from you and give it to someone else. Remember the parable of the talents? (Matthew 25:14–30).

Like Deborah, encourage those who fear, who are discouraged. Faith is contagious, and you might change the life of someone and, in turn, the lives of those around them.

Expect opposition: Satan does not like it when we obey. He will be quick to move to hinder your walk through various tactics.

One being betrayal. Sisera came with all his resources against the Israelites: nine hundred chariots of iron and all the men available (4:13). Not a portion, not the majority. All of them! Obedience causes opposition to soar, and intimidation to come exactly where you are, as close as possible: Barak and Deborah were standing on Mount Tabor. That's precisely where Sisera took his troops at the foot of the mountain.

Last, if do all this, the Lord will fight for you; He is already on the battlefield, Deborah said. All you need to do is, like Sisera, to show up, watch, and finish the work.

In chapter 5, Barak and Deborah sang a psalm of victory together. This song was recorded in writing and shared with future generations to this day. They celebrated the complete triumph over Sisera together. When done, don't forget to thank the Lord, to honor Him, and to spread what He has done in your life—every victory, whether big or small, is worth celebrating and passing down to future generations.

WALK BY FAITH EVERY DAY

"Through wisdom a house is built,
And by understanding it is established;
By knowledge the rooms are filled
With all precious and pleasant riches.

A wise man is strong,
Yes, a man of knowledge increases strength;

For by wise counsel you will wage your own war,
And in a multitude of counselors there is safety.

Wisdom is too lofty for a fool;
He does not open his mouth in the gate" (Proverbs 24:3–7).

REFLECTION QUESTIONS

Do you find yourself in situations sometimes where indecision limits you? How can you step up for the Lord? What can you do today to change your situation?

ABIGAIL, WIFE OF NABAL

Wealth is not inherently bad when it is appropriately managed. It testifies to God's blessings in someone's life, as seen in the cases of King Solomon and Abraham. The question is, what will we do with wealth? The Bible gives examples of many men and women who were very rich at some point in their lives: Abraham was blessed, and he blessed others; Barzillai brought comfort to David in times of distress; and Job was wealthy. He suddenly lost everything; however, his heart was not attached to the riches of this earth, and he was blessed again later. We also have examples of men and women who did not manage their wealth wisely and were controlled by it. If anything, these riches ruled over their hearts. Nabal, in 1 Samuel 25, was one of them. His story sharply contrasts with that of Abigail, his wife, a woman of wisdom and generosity. Their story, and how they managed their wealth, is directly tied to David's story.

Nabal had everything: a beautiful and wise wife, sheep, goats, shearers, a thriving business. Abigail, his wife, owned the same thing with a little extra; she was wise. So, at the beginning, Abigail had almost everything: the brains, the looks, the wealth. However, she was not in a happy marriage and was probably miserable. As with the traditions of the time, she was likely forced into an undesirable marriage by her parents.

Their story goes as follows. David, the future king, fled with his men into the wilderness. He had just lost his spiritual adviser, the prophet Samuel, a man who had walked with David ever since he had been chosen to be king by God. Following this loss, he found himself in the deserts: a natural one (he fled from Saul to hide in the desert) and a spiritual one (no more prophet to advise him). David was then poor, in need, surrounded by men who depended on him for their survival. He was a leader, a warrior, and a good man. Nabal, on the contrary, lived in the city in abundance. He was rich, had servants and shepherds, but he was mean and a scoundrel (1 Samuel 25:15). He blatantly refused to help those in need, humiliating and insulting David and his men at the same time.

Following this rejection and ungratefulness, Nabal's death was resolved in David's heart—death for him and all who belonged to him, including Abigail. At that moment, Abigail found herself in a difficult situation. On one side, she had her husband, her duties of obedience, and respect for him. On the other side,

David and his men were on their way to kill her, even though she was innocent. Her conscience dictated her conduct. Abigail decided to go against her husband's wishes and stepped up to do what was right in God's eyes. That's when she made a difference for herself and everyone in her household.

Let's see how she stood out. First, she didn't fight her position in marriage. She was certainly not happy, despite being smart, surrounded by scoundrels and mean men. She didn't try to escape her situation but took a stand to be rightful and generous. She did not try to create her own miracle by human means, and God intervened in her favor. Later, she became the wife of a king.

When her servants came to inform her of Nabal's behavior, she listened to them and acted upon. She did not dismiss the warnings. They saved her life, and she saved theirs. She found herself stuck between two possibilities: to follow Nabal and the dictates of society of the times, or her conscience. She listened to her conscience, not the voice of men (Nabal), and saved all the house of Nabal from destruction. She blessed David with food when he needed it. She walked to him in humility, on a donkey, providing for his needs and those of his men. She did not consider the cost, the expense, or the possible consequences on her life for disobeying her husband. She was generous in her donation. The Bible says that there were at least six hundred men with David, not counting their families. That's a lot of people to feed!

There is a lot we can learn from Abigail's behavior. Sometimes, when trying to find a solution to our problems, we create new issues that are more difficult to resolve than the original one, or we make the original problems more complex. If nothing you did improved your situation, stop. Come to the Lord, and He will take care of your issues. Abigail was in an unhappy marriage. However, the Lord saw her situation and resolved it. This underscores the importance of seeking God's guidance in all our decisions, big or small.

Abigail's story also teaches us the importance of discernment. The Lord speaks in many ways, and we must be open to His guidance. Even the smallest messenger can deliver a message from the Lord. The servants came to Abigail. Should she have ignored them, they would all be dead by the end of the chapter. Listen to the warnings. Not all voices are from God. Learn to discern, ask the Holy Spirit for the gift of discernment. Don't listen to the Nabal, the naysayers, the overly negative people who will shatter your dreams and hopes. Listen to the still voice of the Lord.

Advice is just that: someone else trying to push their opinion on you. Some are good, some are not. Like with the voices, use discernment when people give you advice; gauge it against the Word of God. Do they follow the Lord's instructions on generosity and trust? Or do they go along with Nabal's words of greed and jealousy? Choose wisely. When making a decision with the Lord in mind, leave the consequences (if any) to Him. Remember Psalm 1:1–3:

> Blessed is the man
> Who walks not in the counsel of the ungodly,

Nor stands in the path of sinners,
Nor sits in the seat of the scornful;
But his delight is in the law of the Lord,
And in His law he meditates day and night.
He shall be like a tree.
Planted by the rivers of water,
That brings forth its fruit in its season,
Whose leaf also shall not wither;
And whatever he does shall prosper.

The story of Abigail and Nabal illustrates two distinct approaches to wealth: Nabal's is to hoard it and flaunt it in the faces of the less fortunate or those in need. Abigail's way is to share and bless those who are unfortunate and in need. The first one led to death. At the end of the story, when Abigail told Nabal she had given food to David for his men, he was so in shock, he died of what could have been a heart attack. When David saw what Abigail had done, he blessed her and asked her to become his wife once she was widowed. Don't let riches ruin your life, but be generous with others.

Nabal and Abigail also show us two ways of answering a cry for help: Nabal's way was to reject it and be ungrateful toward the very same men who protected his flock. Even his servants and shepherds admitted so to Abigail. Abigail responded to the cry for help with food and provisions for all six hundred men and their families. She did not count the cost. She answered the cry for help generously. Be wisely generous; use discernment.

In conclusion, the story of Abigail and Nabal teaches us that there are two ways of facing situations: God's way and man's way. Abigail's intervention saved her life, her husband's, and those of all the servants under her responsibility from the wrath of David. Later, God took care of a very evil man and a scoundrel and blessed Abigail beyond measure. She became the wife of a king, and as she provided for six hundred men for a few days, the Lord provided for her for the rest of her life. She became the wife of a king and beget a son named Daniel. Like Abigail, bless the others, but be wise; they must be genuine. Make discernment and wisdom your daily allies. If you lack something, pray, and it will be given to you.

WALK BY FAITH EVERY DAY

The blessing of the Lord makes one rich, And He adds no sorrow with it" (Proverbs 10:22).

REFLECTION QUESTIONS

Nabal's decisions led David to take extreme measures against him and his family. Everyone was saved because of Abigail. How can you make a difference in your family when sin and danger loom at the door? How can you bless those around you?

A WOMAN OF ABEL OF BETH MAACHAH

Reading: 2 Samuel 20: 16–22

Would you believe me if I said that wisdom can save cities from destruction? Biblical accounts show that it has. At least, it saved all the inhabitants of a town called Abel of Beth Maachah. The wisdom of one woman saved countless lives and prevented the spilling of innocent blood by Joab, King David's general.

How did this happen?

Toward the end of his reign, King David faced many challengers to his right to rule, both internal and external. Following the death of David's son Absalom, who was probably the greatest and most threatening challenger of all, another man named Sheba rose among the people. He called the men of Israel to reject David as king. He was so convincing that all the men of

Israel, except the members of the tribe of Judah, turned away from King David and walked back to their tents and their houses. After this rebellion, King David, already distraught over the Absalom affair (described in 2 Samuel 13 to 19), sent his general Joab in search of Sheba.

Reading through 1 and 2 Samuel, we see that Joab was a man of war and blood, ruthless and without mercy against everything and everyone who stood against King David. After all, he killed Absalom despite David's explicit request to spare his life. And since the city had welcomed an enemy of the crown within its walls, its destruction was set in the mind of Joab.

Fleeing from Joab, Sheba sought refuge in the city of Abel of Beth Maachah, where a wise woman lived. Traditionally, Abel of Beth Maachah was seen as a peaceful city where people came to settle disputes (2 Samuel 20:18–19). However, for some reason, this time, wisdom did not prevail. The city allowed a treacherous and rebellious man to find shelter within its walls. It put its peace and survival in jeopardy when David's general organized the construction of siege ramps around Abel's defensive walls, and all his soldiers began battering the gates and walls to breach them.

However, even if destruction and death were decided in the general's mind, one woman made a difference. We do not know her name, but we do know she was wise. As her city was being besieged, and when everyone was hiding behind the walls, paralyzed by fear, she stood on the wall and faced the problem directly, negotiating with Joab. Eventually, a solution was reached. The rest is history. She rallied all the city residents to follow the proposed plan, and within a short time, the head of Sheba was thrown over the walls to Joab's feet. Joab and his armies left, and Abel of Beth Maachah found peace again. It had come very close to destruction.

King Solomon records an event like that of the town of Abel in Ecclesiastes 9:14–15:

> I also saw under the sun this example of wisdom that greatly impressed me: There was once a small city with only a few people in it. And a powerful king came against it, surrounded it and built huge siege works against it. Now there lived in that city a man poor but wise, and he saved the city by his wisdom. But nobody remembered that poor man. So I said, "Wisdom is better than strength." But the poor man's wisdom is despised, and his words are no longer heeded.

Wisdom is a gift of the Spirit that anyone can receive through prayer. James 1:5 says that "If any of you lacks wisdom, let him ask of God, who gives to all liberally and without reproach, and it will be given to him. But let him ask in faith, with no doubting, for he who doubts is like a wave of the sea driven and tossed by the wind." It may not be the most glamorous or impressive gift, but it is crucial in God's eyes. After all, an entire book of the Old Testament is dedicated to it,[8] and there are probably people

---

8   That would be the book of Proverbs, written by King Solomon.

around who possess the spiritual gift of wisdom. Pray and ask to receive wisdom. Read the book of Proverbs to understand what wisdom is. You will make a difference in your surroundings.

What can we learn from this woman? When rebellion and treason, in one word, sin, enter your house because a door was left open, you face the same two choices as the city of Abel: You can either let sin stay, or you can remove it and throw it out. If you continue to sin against your king in secret and shelter it, sin will grow. It will corrupt everyone around, disturb your peace, and bring death to your door (impersonated here by Joab). However, if you decide to eliminate it from your life and your home, you will regain a sense of life and peace.

Don't fight only for yourself, and don't fight alone. The wise woman gathered the city's inhabitants and convinced them of the right course of action for their peace and security. Fight alongside your allies in prayer for everyone around you and within your circle of influence, your walls. The actions and wisdom given by God can, and will, make a difference. You will bring many to life and restore peace. People will seek your presence and your advice.

In conclusion, seeking wisdom does not bring fame or glory. You probably won't perform on a stage in front of crowds, nor will you likely amass millions in your bank account. However, you will make a difference in the lives of those around you. You will stand at the crossroads of life and death, speaking life to an audience that is heading toward death. Wisdom will guide your decisions and influence future generations because true wisdom comes from God.

WALK BY FAITH EVERY DAY

"But the wisdom that is from above is first pure, then peaceable, gentle, willing to yield, full of mercy and good fruits, without partiality and without hypocrisy. Now the fruit of righteousness is sown in peace by those who make peace" (James 3:17–18).

REFLECTION QUESTIONS

How can wisdom help you in your daily activities? What are the advantages of being filled with the gist of wisdom? What can you do today to receive this gift if you think you need more wisdom in your life?

PART 10

Those Who Worked in the Shadows

Illustration 10: Luke

On one side are the generals whom everybody knows, follows, and admires. On the other side are the soldiers, the privates who are known by their matricula. They are the ones nobody knows except their family and friends. Nobody follows them, admires them, agrees with them, or disagrees with them. They carry out orders. However, an army of generals alone will not win a war. They can send all the orders they want, but if there is no one on the other end of the chain of command, those orders will go nowhere. Those who work in the shadows are essential for victory; they are the hands, the feet, of the army—the ones who do the work, the execution. They might not have international recognition, but they can make a profound impact and leave a legacy that could change everything. A single act of courage can transform the world. These shadow soldiers are the Josephs of Arimathea, the Lukes, the Ananiases. We are all these soldiers.

LUKE

Reading: Gospel According to Luke and book of Acts.,
Colossians 4:14, Philemon v.24, 2 Timothy 4:11

Many dream of being remembered by future generations, leaving a mark, and influencing the world. Unfortunately, most will be forgotten unless they leave a legacy that changes the world. The dream of every author is to write a book that will last and make an impact, but very few accomplish both. Luke the Evangelist was one of those rare individuals. Despite his vast and impactful influence, Luke remains a humble figure. His modesty is inspiring, as he probably never imagined that his letters would shape our knowledge and understanding of the Church and the Holy Spirit two thousand years later.

Little is known about the identity and life of Luke the Evangelist. However, the mystery surrounding him only adds to his allure. We can learn from history and the writings of Paul and Luke about how to leave a lasting legacy and influence our generation and the ones to come. Luke was a man who successfully wore many hats and managed multiple careers at once; yet, he used his skills to build the Kingdom of God.

Nothing in Luke's upbringing foreshadowed the impact he would have on the world or the extraordinary journeys he would undertake as a follower of a man named Paul. Luke grew up as one of the anonymous among others, lost among the crowds visiting Antioch, Syria, where, according to history, Luke was born. Located roughly three hundred miles north of Jerusalem, Antioch was the third-largest city in the Roman Empire. It was a wealthy city situated at the crossroads of major trade routes, where caravans from the east, west, north, and south converged. The city was prosperous and cosmopolitan. Luke was used to enjoying life in the Hellenistic way—focused on pleasure, happiness, self-control, virtue, and rational thought—and probably following one of the many philosophies popular at the time, such as Stoicism and Epicureanism.

The inhabitants of Antioch worshipped wealth and material success, and Luke's family was probably no exception. He was raised in a pagan Greek culture that worshipped idols and engaged in religious activities. Nearby Antioch was a temple dedicated to Apollo, the Greek/Roman god who drove the sun across the sky every day, and was associated with music, dance, healing, and illness. Apollo embodied ideals of beauty, truth, and order, which were reflected in the management and daily life of the city, as well as in its thriving artistic and scientific endeavors. Luke worked as a physician, a logical pursuit when living in the town of Apollo. He was an educated man who studied medicine under the mentorship of other physicians.

One day, among the many travelers that passed through the city, a man named Paul came in preaching a different kind of philosophy and approach to life. This new teaching contradicted everything Antioch had to offer, and it completely transformed Luke's life. He found himself facing the Truth and Life. He abandoned the pagan ways to become a follower of Christ, a Christian, as they were first called in Antioch. This transformation, from a life of paganism marked by wealth and pleasure to a life of service and faith, is a testament to the power of the Holy Spirit and the truth to change lives.

From that moment, his life was transformed. He left behind a comfortable pagan life adorned with wealth and pleasures, driven by the pursuit of success, with the prospects of a successful and respected career as a physician, to become a traveler, often unsure where to sleep or where his next meal would come from and wondering if a riot would soon break out over the teachings of Paul. These new circumstances did not stop Luke. Through the dangers of being on the road, he also became a historian and an investigative writer. He is the author of the third Gospel and the book of Acts of the apostles. He narrated the travels of Paul, the work of the apostles, the ministry of Jesus Christ, the birth of John the Baptist, and the ascension of Jesus to Heaven. He details how the Gospel first began to spread in Jerusalem, then in Judea, and ultimately to the ends of the world. His writings were carefully researched. He used previous texts as a basis (probably Mark) and interviewed firsthand eyewitnesses such as Mary, the mother of Jesus. As a doctor, he focused a lot on the miracles Jesus performed. He also masterfully described the humanity of the Savior and the role women played in serving Jesus.

He became an itinerant evangelist. Luke joined Paul during the second missionary journey and participated in Paul's third and final trip from Jerusalem to Rome. He wrote accounts of his journeys to participate in the teachings and spread of the Gospel during his time and after. So, being the faithful companion, he was jailed with Paul, shipwrecked in Malta. He witnessed Paul's beating and stoning. Despite all this, he remained faithful because the message he was responsible for carrying brought truth and salvation to thousands. His dedication to spreading the Gospel, even in the face of adversity, is a powerful example of the impact of faith and service.

While Luke's exact ethnicity is a matter of debate among historians, it is generally believed that he was a Greek Gentile. This means that he was not Jewish. If Luke were indeed a Greek Gentile, he would be the only non-Jew included in the New Testament canon of authors. This unique perspective allowed him to present the Gospel in a way that was accessible to a broader audience, making his contributions to the New Testament particularly significant.

He died in Greece at age eighty-four, having lived a life of service and faith. His death marked the end of a remarkable journey, but his legacy continues to inspire and guide us today.

A lot can be learned when considering what others say about a person. In Luke's case, we have the direct account of Apostle Paul in three of his epistles: Colossians, Philemon, and 2 Timothy. Paul esteems Luke highly in his writings. He refers to Luke as the beloved physician and his coworker, seeing him as an equal and a person who completes the same work. As Apostle Paul neared death, he reflected on his life, his struggle for truth, and his efforts to spread the Gospel. He probably faced moments of solitude when those around him chose to leave or go their own way. Luke, the beloved physician, remained with Paul. In his second epistle to Timothy, Paul's words, "Only Luke is with me," reflect Luke's unwavering loyalty and faithfulness.

On the medical side, God first provided for Paul's physical and medical needs by placing a physician near him during his travels. Paul endured a lot of physical persecution, such as being beaten. Luke likely utilized his medical skills and talents to care for Paul after these events. We also know that Paul suffered from an undisclosed thorn in the flesh that could have necessitated the support of a physician.

As we read the two texts by Luke, we see that they were directed at only one reader, named Theophilus, to present a defense for the faith and the ministry of Paul. However, these two texts have profoundly influenced the world and billions of humans. Imagine what Christianity would be like today if we did not have those writings. What would the world be like? We would have no information about the miraculous birth of John the Baptist, no mention of the conversion of Zacchaeus, no description of the *Via Dolorosa* (Luke 23:27–31), no knowledge of how the baptism in the Holy Spirit first occurred, and no information about Pentecost.

Luke was the man who never spoke but only reported what the others did and said. He stood aside, followed, and cared (being with Paul, he probably prayed for the sick and preached the Good News to the Gentiles as well). He was the one no one noticed but Paul. However, he has been pivotal in our knowledge and understanding of Jesus Christ and the Gospel because God knew and saw this man's faithfulness, loyalty, and genuine heart.

Like Luke, today, disciples can influence and change the world. By addressing one person, millions can be saved in the long run. Jesus' disciples don't work alone; they are part of a larger army, fighting in a plan that involves many in both space and time. Like Luke, you live in a world adorned with pleasure, sin, idols, and philosophies. Like Luke, even if you are in this world, you are not part of it.

Learn from Luke that every little contribution can have a significant impact if we remember that we are not working for ourselves, but for the glory of the Lord and the salvation of lost souls. Your testimony, your salvation story, can change your family tree and your work environment, because the Holy Spirit Luke talked about is still at work today. Spread the truth; it will set you and others free. Life with God is worth living. Life without God is doomed to death and boredom. I am not saying it will be easy. Meeting Paul certainly changed Luke's life and destiny—the young man probably never imagined he would be shipwrecked in Malta. But it is the only life worth living.

Standing aside doesn't mean doing nothing. Luke probably never imagined his writing would still be around two thousand years later, changing the world and influencing the lives of millions. He never sought glory, nor boasted of his skills, nor claimed to be accounted with Apostle Paul. He served at this level. He contributed and used his skills for the Lord, and we live in the legacy of his work today.

Thrive to do the same.

WALK BY FAITH EVERY DAY

"And whatever you do, do it heartily, as to the Lord and not to men, knowing that from the Lord you will receive the reward of the inheritance; for you serve the Lord Christ" (Colossians 3:23).

REFLECTION QUESTIONS

You were born with a purpose and talents. You have developed skills and talents over the years that enable you to accomplish work for the Lord. What do you know, or what skills do you possess, that you can use for God? Are you a person of words? A people person? An organizer? God can use everything if you are willing to become His soldier and servant.

Think about the legacy you will leave or want to leave to your children and your family. What can you do today to build this legacy and positively impact the generations that follow?

JOSEPH OF ARIMATHEA

Reading: Matthew 27:57–60; Mark 15:42–47; Luke 23:50–56; and John 18:38–42

During the time of Jesus, there once was a group of seventy-one men in Jerusalem who wielded so much influence that they could sway the decision of the governor of Judea and command Roman soldiers to execute fellow residents of the city. This council, known as the Sanhedrin, was so powerful it was not advisable to oppose or disagree with it. Facing their power and prestige was like trying to stop a modern road roller moving at full speed; you could get hurt or even crushed. However, the Bible tells of a man who stood up to these rulers and religious leaders. His actions are recorded in all four Gospels and are remembered to this day. His name was Joseph.

Joseph is described in the Gospels as a wealthy man from Arimathea, a city approximately twenty miles northwest of

Jerusalem. He was a respected member of the Sanhedrin, belonging to the Judeans' upper class and elites. The Sanhedrin was a Jewish supreme court and council based in Jerusalem, led by the high priest. Its powers and influence were significant, affecting every aspect of Jewish life in Judea; they enforced civil and religious law and interpreted sacred texts. Additionally, they possessed the authority to impose capital punishment—a power they used to condemn Jesus Christ. Beyond its civil duties, the Sanhedrin convened in a chamber within the Temple in Jerusalem known as the Chamber of Hewn Stones. It is believed that this council originated from the Council of the Seventy Elders, established by Moses in Numbers 11:16–30, which added to its social prestige as a religious authority, as the seventy elders shared Moses' spirit at the time of its creation. To be chosen for the Sanhedrin, a man had to demonstrate his Jewish lineage, be at least forty years old, have thoroughly studied the Torah throughout his life, be well-versed in both scriptures and oral traditions, be physically fit, and stand out from others. Joseph of Arimathea possessed all the influence, prestige, and authority associated with this court. As a result, he wielded considerable influence, was seen as a role model, and was trusted by the public, with expectations of specific behavior.

However, his decisions and actions became highly controversial when he publicly revealed himself as a secret disciple of Jesus Christ and took a stand against the court's rulings, risking everything he owned and believed in.

Joseph of Arimathea dwelt in the shadows and was a secret disciple of Jesus Christ (John 19), waiting for the Kingdom of God to come. According to Luke, he stood out one day by disagreeing with the court's decision to condemn Jesus Christ to capital punishment, and later took care of the body of Jesus Christ with the help of Nicodemus. After the crucifixion, and before the Sabbath began, he went, in sight of all, to Pilate and asked for the body of Jesus Christ. He, then, took it from the cross himself, and after wrapping the body in linen he had purchased, he bound it and placed it in his own tomb. By doing so, Joseph of Arimathea became a model of faith and righteousness. He stood in opposition to an official religious council for what was right. Imagine this one man standing alone, facing another group of seventy or so men defending what was, in their eyes, a criminal. There is nothing more dangerous than a religious crowd driven and motivated by religious motives and hate. He set aside traditions and religiosity to choose truth.

On a personal level, it is written in John 19:38–42 that Joseph of Arimathea, helped by Nicodemus, took Jesus from the cross. Between the thirty-nine lashes, the crowns of thorns, the carrying of the cross, the crucifixion, and being pierced with a spear, we can say that there was not much left of a human body after the Roman torture. Specialists agree that Jesus' body was covered in blood. According to Numbers 19 11–13, anyone who touched a dead body was considered unclean for seven days and had to undergo purification rituals. Joseph was a Pharisee, well-versed in the Law. Still, he chose to do what was right over his purification because his love for the truth overcame his religious engagement. His action transcended all social order—crucifixion was primarily used against people of lower social status, such as slaves, pirates, non-citizens, political and religious agitators, or disgraced soldiers. By wrapping Jesus' body in linen cloth that Joseph had bought, he associated himself with a "criminal" who had been condemned to the crucifixion (Mark 16:20).

His actions after the crucifixion became a public act of religious disobedience, but still an act of love for God's Word and Kingdom. He took Jesus' body off the cross, touching a dead person, a criminal, which came against the Mosaic law. As a religious man, a Pharisee, and a member of the council, he went against the rules and regulations of each one of these groups.

But his actions go beyond the simple personal act and decision. He prevented the land from being cursed because, according to Deuteronomy 21:22–23, every man put to death for a crime should not be left hanging on a tree, or God would curse him, and the land would be defiled. Joseph knew the Law and worked to protect his people from adding a crime to that of crucifying an innocent.

The secret disciple became a public defender of Jesus Christ by taking the body of Jesus from the cross and paying for his burial. He put Jesus in his own tomb (Matthew 27:60), which all the members of the Sanhedrin knew since they had asked for the tomb to be guarded and blocked by a stone.

What can we learn from Joseph of Arimathea today? Several ideas presented in his testimony are applicable to daily life. The first one is that religion and religiosity will try to kill truth. It's the fellow religious men who condemned Jesus to death. We see it today, the post-modernist[9] philosophy that took over the world in the middle of the twentieth century claims that there are no absolutes and that truth is relative to each one's experience. The Bible tells us the contrary. It teaches that there is one truth found in Jesus Christ. Debates are not held around the dining table on Thanksgiving day only, anymore. But they are everywhere: in the public arena, the political sphere, under a family roof. Like Joseph, it has become difficult not to be confronted when presenting ideas of absolute truth. Take courage and stand up for Jesus and the truth. Let what is right and what aligns with your conscience guide you, even if it means going against the general flow. In today's world, the anti-conformists are not who they used to be; Christians and those who hold on to the truth as universal have become the anti-conformists of society. Trends are ideas that propagate like fire; however, it does not make them right. The faster trends or ideologies appear, the faster they often disappear.

------

9   Post-Modernism is a philosophy that was born during the middle of the twentieth century. It came in opposition to Modernism, another philosophy that was born of the eighteenth-century Enlightenment and that claim that science and reason were the absolute the explanation of everything. Philosophers, authors, and others, seeing the failures of Modernism with all the wars that plagued the nineteenth and twentieth centuries, came in opposition and claim, today, that everything is relative, a matter of interpretation, and that there are no absolutes, that only personal experience matters. It holds a great distrusts of grand theories and ideologies, and objective or absolute truths. It is widespread in our universities today, in art, literature, and has now reached the political circles. Deconstruction is one of the techniques used to establish post-Modernism, and it claims that reality is a social construct.

Joseph also invested his own money in the truth. It is one thing to believe in an idea. It is another thing to act on it. It is even more meaningful to invest your money in it. You never know what God can do with your investments!

Next, he took the body down himself. Do things yourself, don't wait or expect others to do what is in your heart. You might be the only one to care. He did not receive an order from an angel; he acted out of love and faith.

We don't hear about him anywhere else in the Gospels. Glory was not what he sought; however, God considered his actions worthy of being remembered and recorded by all the Gospel writers. His love for the truth was evident in his actions, his behavior in the public eye, and his investments. Very few events have found their way into the four texts!

WALK BY FAITH EVERY DAY

"And do not be conformed to this world, but be transformed by the renewing of your mind, that you may prove what is that good and acceptable and perfect will of God" (Romans 12:2).

REFLECTION QUESTIONS

How did Joseph of Arimathea take a stand for God? Do you think it was difficult? Dangerous? How can you take a stand for God today? What can help you grow your faith and courage to take a stand?

ANANIAS

Reading: Acts 9:10-19

Typically, people are familiar with the famous generals of God, people such as Billy Graham, David Wilkerson, and Charles Finney. These men had a significant impact on a world scale. But few know or remember the men and women who led these men to Christ, trained them in the Word, or raised them in the faith. In a sense, these behind-the-scenes actors have an impact as significant as those who stand on the frontstage because without them, without their testimony, their persistence in seeing this child grow in the knowledge of God, this young man developing his evangelist ministry, there would be no Billy Graham, no David Wilkerson, no Charles Finney.

In the Bible, few individuals have had as profound an impact on world history as Ananias. I am not talking about Sapphira's husband but the other one. Ananias' obedience changed the course of world history. Like the other heroes in the Bible, his name is not among the most illustrious. He does not figure in Hebrews 11. Apart from these nine verses in Acts 9, we do not hear about the disciple of Damascus, except perhaps on one other occasion, when the apostle Paul shares his testimony.

Ananias was a simple man from Damascus, an anonymous man who had become a disciple of Jesus Christ. In his faithfulness, God chose him and invested him with a special mission that would change the course of history and transform the world forever: He was tasked with restoring Paul's vision and introducing the man who persecuted the church and approved Stephen's martyrdom as a new disciple to the other believers in Damascus.

However, he was not chosen by mistake; the Lord knew what He was doing when He sent Ananias to Paul. To begin, Ananias was a disciple of Jesus Christ and was known as such. His lifestyle reflected his beliefs, as he lived according to Jesus' teachings in every aspect of his life. As such, God knew his faithfulness. Ananias was also a man of prayer and vision. He was in prayer when the Lord came to him, asking him to visit Paul. He discerned the Lord's voice because he could answer His call without being mistaken: "Here I am, Lord" (Acts 9:10). He obeyed in every detail despite well-founded fears. Paul's evil reputation was well-established all over Judea and preceded him everywhere he went. Ananias really had to have faith that the Lord sent him to meet Saul of Tarsus in the name of Jesus Christ.

Additionally, Ananias was well-versed in miracles and healing. When he laid his hands on Paul, he restored sight to the blind man through his faith in Jesus Christ. He walked daily in the miraculous and the supernatural.

He didn't let revenge or anger control him, nor did he seek personal justice. When he faced Saul, weak and blind, at his mercy, he didn't indulge in triumphalism or lecture him about his past actions and accusations of deserving what had happened. Instead, he brought Saul of Tarsus into the light and baptism. He called the enemy "My brother," and, as a true disciple of Jesus Christ, he loved the enemy even before this person showed any signs of change. Ananias' humility in this moment serves as a powerful example for us all.

Today, Ananiases are everywhere. We don't see or hear about them. Quietly, they pray for someone they meet who is sick or in need. They walk in faith wherever they go. Even if others don't notice or acknowledge their works, the Lord does, and He remembers them. I don't think Ananias requested that these verses be included in Luke's writings. I believe Luke knew Paul's testimony and judged it worthy to add the name of the man who conquered the fear engendered by a man's reputation, to go and bring him to salvation.

Like Ananias, be men and women of faith who will discern the voice of the Lord, walk in faith, and change the world. Do not seek your own justice or revenge. Leave it all to God. Pray to receive wisdom and the other gifts of the Spirit. Be faithful in prayer, faith, and hope. You don't know what the Lord can do with your prayers and how they can impact the world.

Without Ananias, there might not have been an Apostle Paul. We would not read two-thirds of the New Testament. Perhaps the Lord would have sent someone to him. Still, the effect would not have been the same because Saul had seen in a vision "a man named Ananias, who came in and laid his hands on him, that he might recover his sight" (Acts 9:12). It had to be Ananias who prayed for Saul, and his actions had a profound impact on Paul's conversion.

As soon as his mission was completed, Saul started preaching in the synagogues (Acts 9:20). Presumably, Ananias was among the disciples who helped Paul escape from Damascus shortly afterward (Acts 9:25).

Another man played a key role in Paul's conversion; his name was Judas (not Judas, who betrayed Jesus!). He is the one who took Paul into his house and sheltered him despite his bad reputation. He went against all tides, all beliefs, and believed Ananias' testimony when he said that Paul had changed. Ananias' bold actions created a domino effect that encouraged others to do the same.

Ananias and Judas are still needed in the Kingdom today. People who don't seek recognition or applause for every small act will follow the words of Jesus Christ, with His glory in mind alone. Humility and selflessness are vital virtues that we should live by and demonstrate in our service to the Lord.

WALK BY FAITH EVERY DAY

"And let us not grow weary while doing good, for in due season we shall reap if we do not lose heart. Therefore, as we have opportunity, let us do good to all, especially to those who are of the household of faith" (Galatians 6: 9–10).

REFLECTION QUESTIONS

How can you make a difference in someone's life and faith today? How can keeping the glory of God in mind and as a motivator for your decisions change you, others, or the world?

PART 11

Those Who Defied Empires

Illustration 11: Yokebed

Standing alone, confronting giants, holding rain, parting seas, all these events appear at least once in the Bible. They all have one thing in common: They display the exercise of an unmovable faith and the belief that God is greater. Doing what is right may be less impressive, is not easy either, but imagine taking a stand against an empire and defying the king's evil orders? Many in the Bible did exactly that. Most are well-known: Moses. Elijah, Daniel. Others are less known, but their stand still changed the future of their people. These are Shiphrah and Puah, Yokebed, Miriam, Jephthah, and Jael and Heber. They truly turned the world upside down.

SHIPHRAH AND PUAH

Reading: Exodus 1:15–21

Choosing to do what is right seems obvious when we hear about situations that are far away or in which we are not directly involved or concerned. It's another ordeal to act on that decision when we are directly facing the situation, especially if one's life and survival are at stake! This first chapter in Exodus illustrates a compelling example of "Taking God's side" and shows how to be courageous in the face of evil! It brings to light a group of women, the Israel midwives, who fearlessly championed what was right. Their audacious act of defying Pharaoh's orders and preserving the lives of the male children stands as a powerful testament to their steadfast faith and courage.

As they were doing their job, one day, Shiphrah and Puah received an order coming directly from the throne to kill all the baby boys born among Israel that they would deliver. They refused to obey this evil law, and as a result, they found themselves in a dangerous situation that could have cost them their lives. However, Pharaoh was not the only one to notice their refusal to obey. God saw their courage. As a result, the Bible says that He blessed them and their families for the decision they took to protect the baby boys.

In the midst of turmoil, these women remained humble and unknown. They made a difference at the time for the Israelis. They stood alone against evil, protecting life. By their professional activity, they were bearers of life and could not bring themselves to take an innocent life. They embraced their duty and, through their profession, they aided in childbirth. The Bible declares, "The fear of the Lord is the beginning of wisdom" (Proverbs 9:10).

These women had the fear of God: Pharaoh was a powerful king who ruled over what was, at the time, the greatest empire of the Orient. The empire is responsible for the construction of the pyramids and other magnificent buildings along the Nile River. He had the power of life and death over his people. Pharaoh was also considered a god. In this matter, we see two divinities in competition: a false god, a man born like everyone else who claims to be a god and who believes in all kinds of other divinities, and the real God, the Creator. These women stood against false religion and beliefs by taking God's side. These women did what was right: These orders are horrible. Despite the consequences, the women stood for life by protecting innocent people. They even lied to the Pharaoh about deliveries. They were driven by selflessness and a deep sense of duty, and expected nothing in return for their actions. And yet, God, in His infinite wisdom, blessed them and their families for their noble deeds.

Like Shiphrah and Puah, you are called to breathe life into those around us who are spiritually dead, blind, wounded, or lost. You are here to take a stand and say stop to Satan, that his tricks and lies are over. Call for the lives and salvation of those around you through prayer and intercession. Be animated by the love of truth and God's glory, not personal gain and power. You are not building your own kingdom, you are not developing your own branded product, or establishing a culture for which you define the elements. Everything you do, do as unto the Lord. Let excellence drive you to do the best in representing and presenting God to those around you. Keep eternity in mind, and you will be even more focused on the present's issues and salvation.

Shiphrah and Puah don't feature in the Faith Hall of Fame of Hebrews 11. This is a powerful reminder that God values our service for His sake, not personal glory. Anonymous individuals perform many heroic actions. Our focus should be on pleasing God, not seeking recognition from man. As Jesus said, your left hand should ignore what your right hand does (Matthew 6:3). God sees your motivations, your secret desires, and your thoughts. We are transparent before Him. Sometimes in life, you are or will be confronted with difficult choices. Your faith will be tested. Be wise in handling things and keep God's interest first.

WALK BY FAITH EVERY DAY

"Commit your way to the Lord,
Trust also in Him,
And He shall bring it to pass" (Psalms 37:5).

REFLECTION QUESTIONS

These two midwives took a stand between life and death. How can you do the same today in your life? In your family's life? How can you breathe life in those around you who are spiritually dead or engaged on a path of death?

How can you demonstrate courage when facing a difficult situation?

YOKEBED

Moses' mother took extraordinary risks to save her son. Indeed, he had been condemned to a horrible death: to be thrown in the Nile River, like every other Israeli baby boy born in Egypt at that time. Pharaoh pronounced this terrible decision to protect his power.

Instead, Yokebed hid him for three months, openly disobeying the orders of the most powerful man of the time. Imagine the anguish this mother lived with and the fear of being discovered. These parents risked capital punishment by hiding a baby from the wrath of Pharaoh. How do you hide the baby's cries or feed him without being seen by soldiers on the alert? The anguish of seeing the fruit of her womb thrown to the Nile among the crocodiles or drowning in muddy waters as the Egyptian soldiers were running by, searching house after house. But Yokebed remitted herself and her child's life to the Lord. After three months, she left the child in a basket in the Nile River, and the Lord took care of him. In a sense, she did what Pharaoh wanted, but on her own terms. She first and foremost trusted the Lord. Not only was the child saved, but as a reward for her faith, she was invited to become the caretaker of her son and received compensation for doing so. The Lord provided for their needs and protected the child by placing him under the responsibility of Pharaoh's sister. From her disobedience to the king of Egypt and her trust in the Lord, the Savior of Israel was born and raised to bring deliverance to Israel. Out of this act of courage, three character traits emerge that inspire us today:

Yokebed feared the Lord. She did not submit to Pharaoh's orders. She trusted her son's life with her Lord, and He honored her faith. For three months, she didn't know where this would take her and her son, but the Lord turned death into life. The baby who was supposed to be killed lived and brought life and freedom to Israel. This is a testament to the power and faithfulness of our God, who can turn even the most dire situations into opportunities for life and freedom.

Sometimes, we act in secret, but the Lord knows. Yokebed hid her son; no doubt her husband Amram helped her. They worked together. There is a sudden sense of accountability when we realize that the Lord sees everything, even if no one else does. Our acts of courage will pass unnoticed to most, even those who are closest. But it is the unknown acts of bravery that built the Lord's Kingdom.

This woman did what was right and acted unselfishly. She made the right decisions at the right time and protected life when everything around her was proclaiming death. We don't hear much about her in the rest of the book, but without her decision to preserve life, we would not have had Moses and all the incredible testimonies that accompanied him and the people of Israel.

Fear the Lord first; respect Him as the Father and Creator He is.

You don't know where today's decisions will take you and your family, nor do you know what your actions will bring. However, you can be sure that God is with you if you trust and obey Him. He knows everything. He has the answers to your questions and the solutions to your problems. Trusting and obeying God is the surest way to find security and guidance in your life.

The Lord will fight for you if you rely on Him. Like Yokebed, take a stand; she defied Pharaoh's orders, army, and tricks to do what was right in the eyes of the Lord. Let Him be your compass and the referee when you face difficult decisions. She was a mother who wanted to save her baby. Remember that the Pharaoh allowed Israel to leave after the death of all the firstborn sons of Egypt, including his.

WALK BY FAITH EVERY DAY

"Trust in the Lord with all your heart,
And lean not on your own understanding;

In all your ways acknowledge Him,
And He shall direct your paths" (Proverbs 3:5–6).

REFLECTION QUESTIONS

Yokebed demonstrated courage and protected life when it was at stake. She hid her baby and he became the guide to Israel and one of the most preeminent figures of the Old testament. Consider something you did today. Either an action or a decision needs to be made. How can this simple act of taking God's side affect the future? Yours, and the ones around you?

MIRIAM

The Domino Effect, also known as the Ripple Effect, occurs when one event triggers a series of subsequent events related to the original one, much like dominoes falling one after another. One good action can set off a chain of reactions we will never know about. At least, not here, not now. It also says that one small step taken today can have a bigger impact tomorrow. Yokebed's choice (mentioned in the previous chapter) started a Domino Effect that resulted in the liberation of Israel from the yoke of the Egyptians. If Yokebed is the first domino, Miriam, her daughter, indeed was the second one. The story of Moses could have ended like this: Pharaoh's sister rescues the baby from the waters. However, this could not have happened without Miriam's courage. Even the smallest acts of faith can have a profound impact, triggering a chain reaction of blessings and salvation.

At the time of the events mentioned in Exodus 1, Miriam was still a child. She was the sister of Aaron and Moses, a Levite born in Egypt, and she experienced the life of the Hebrews under Egyptian rule. Miriam is best remembered today for her rebellion against her brother, the leprosy that followed, or the song of liberation that accompanied the crossing of the Red Sea. She witnessed all the Ten Plagues of Egypt, the Parting of the Red Sea, and the daily bread falling from Heaven. None of this would have been possible without her, who, as a young girl, took a step to watch her baby brother floating in a basket above the turbulent waters of the muddy Nile River. She was not very old when she watched over Moses as he floated on the Nile, and the waters probably reached her waist fast, but do we really understand the implications? This young girl showed great courage in protecting her baby brother. Just like her mother, she defied the Egyptian empire and hid her little brother for the first few months. However, after that, when Yokebed decided it was time to give the baby to the Lord, she followed him into the Nile to see what would happen and to protect him if necessary. She walked the waters infested with crocodiles, mosquitoes, and snakes. She walked through mud, reeds, and the uncertainty of the Nile River, which was still wild and untamed in those days, infested with parasites and other bacteria. She waited patiently for the moment to step into the light, keeping a close eye on the basket. Finally, when the time was right, she emerged from hiding to stand before Pharaoh's sister and make an extraordinary proposal: to find her a nanny for the baby. There may have already been women in Pharaoh's palace whose job was to raise royal children. Still, this proposal found favor with Pharaoh's sister, and Miriam reunited the baby with its mother. It allowed God's plan to be accomplished. Miriam's courage is a beacon of inspiration, showing us that even in the face of great danger, we can stand up for what is right. You can follow her example in your everyday life. You might find yourself working in the shadows, unnoticed by anyone, yet you remain faithful in your work and your faith. You are watching over your children, your family, and your employees, ensuring they are okay. You might be the one who thinks about everyone else, and no one notices. But you are there, and you make sure everything is turning round. Know this: You are making a difference, whether you know it or not.

Muddy waters and snakes will try to discourage you from moving forward; people with good intentions, difficulties, trials, or just life can feel muddy at times. You don't know where you are going, and reeds are hiding your sight. However, keep your eyes on the prize and keep walking, because God is with you. He knows what you are doing. He will reward your faithfulness, even when it remains hidden from human views. Act as if you are doing everything for God, knowing that a small act of kindness can go a long way.

The day you are called to come out of the shadows, whether you are hiding by choice or managing everything from behind, you will step and stand before the Judgment seat of Christ, and all your actions will pass through fire.

The salvation of the Hebrews was the result of the choices made by four women, the last of whom was Miriam. Like links in a chain, they made God's plan of salvation for Israel possible. Their actions, seemingly isolated, were never without consequences. They set off a series of events that interconnect with others and ultimately lead to something greater than themselves—a result they may never fully comprehend or witness. Miriam's role in this was crucial, as she was the one who ensured Moses was reunited with his mother, thus preserving his identity and enabling him to fulfill his destiny. Just as Miriam played a significant role in the salvation of the Hebrews, you too have the potential to make a substantial impact on others through your faith and obedience.

Remember, in your journey of faith, you are not alone. God is with you, guiding your steps and rewarding your faithfulness. You can take comfort in His presence, knowing that He is always there, even when you may feel isolated or unseen.

WALK BY FAITH EVERY DAY

"But those who wait on the Lord
Shall renew their strength;
They shall mount up with wings like eagles,
They shall run and not be weary,
They shall walk and not faint" (Isaiah 40:31).

REFLECTION QUESTIONS

Do you sometimes feel that you are fighting your battles alone? Or that what you do won't make a difference? Know that these are lies of the enemy. God can use you and what you have been doing from behind for the greater plan of salvation.

JEPHTHAH

Not everyone begins life on an equal footing. Starting well is ideal and fortunate; however, not everyone gets that chance. Familial and cultural background set the stage for one's upbringing. Jephthah certainly did not start his life well, and it was not through his own fault. Everything around him was flawed, and nothing indicated he would become a great judge in Israel, following in the steps of Deborah or Gideon. Still, the Lord saw things differently. As Jephthah became obedient and filled with the Spirit, he turned into a vessel of great victories and freedom for the children of Israel, who had been suffering under the hands of the Philistines and the Ammonites for eighteen years.

From a family perspective, Jephthah was conceived and born in sin. He was the biological child of Gilead, a married man, and an unknown prostitute. Gilead had other sons with his wife, who cast away Jephthah after their father died. He should not inherit with them.

From a cultural perspective, Jephthah was born and raised during the time of the Judges, when the Israelites did as they pleased. They were supposed to follow God's Law willingly. However, the reality was different; they repeatedly walked away from the Lord, falling into idolatry. From the one God who saved them from Egypt and parted the Red Sea, they switched to worshiping many gods borrowed from the surrounding cultures. The Bible states that they began to worship the Baals, Astarte, the gods of Syria, Sidon, Moab, Ammon, and the Philistines. One God was not sufficient. Two were not enough either, so they tried every divinity available around them, but none could satisfy them. From a political perspective, one of the consequences of abandoning God and His Law was to be subjected to invasions and persecutions by neighboring groups. Those very civilizations that Israel flirted with became invaders. They attacked the children of Israel, stole their harvest, destroyed their houses, and besieged their cities. The Bible says that "Israel was severely distressed" because of them (Judges 10:9).

So, Jephthah grew up in an atmosphere of untamed religious greed and idolatry, marked by constant defeat and political instability. However, the rest of the story reveals that he did not fall into the traps of the false gods and chose to separate himself from their lies. His life choices influenced everyone around him and led the children of Israel to freedom.

Jephthah stood out from the general trend that plagued the Israelite society. To begin with, he did not allow his hectic familial situation to define who he was when his brothers rejected him. He fled to the land of Tob, a desert area, and began a new life. While in Tob, there was not much he could do against his brothers or the people of the city. His mother was a prostitute. There, as he is learning to rely on the Lord, men gathered around him. Together, they went on incursions. He discovered and trained in the art of leadership and warfare. He built a reputation.

As God refused to deliver the children of Israel, they sought a human solution. They found Jephthah, whose renown as a leader and a military commander, having been victorious repeatedly, had grown and spread. Apart from him, no man was able to lead Israel to freedom because they were all in the bondage of Satan. Jephthah had fled away from the idolatry of the children of Israel and was not contaminated by it. He was set apart. And when the time came for him to step up, he did. However, Jephthah answered the distressed call of the Gileadites, under one condition: that he would become their leader and fulfill the role of a judge in the biblical sense. But answering the call was not the only good decision he made. Soon after meeting with the leaders of Gilead, he went to Mizpah and reported everything to the Lord. What the men of Gilead did not do, he did. With the Lord's approval, he became the leader—his first decision as a commander was to contact the king of the Ammonites and ask for the reasons behind the incursions. Hearing the lies from the Ammonite king, Jephthah restored the truth and questioned the real motives behind the king's actions. Once the truth was reset, he went to war and led the troops to complete victory.

There is a lot we can learn from Jephthah. From a personal perspective, self-perception is often defined by how others perceive us, rather than how God sees us. Our vision of the self is tainted. Ego, self-righteousness, low self-esteem, the opinions others have of us, and what they say about us, all act as a screen that impedes our understanding of who we really are. Too often, we define ourselves through the eyes of others. But do we allow God to define who we are? And do we see ourselves through His lens? If we examine the story of Jephthah, the Bible describes him as a mighty man of valor—a hero. Although he was perceived as an outcast, an illegitimate child by his brothers, the Lord saw his heart and his valor. In His eyes, he was the man who would deliver the children of Israel from the yoke and the burden of the invasions. Do not let others define who you are. Do not define yourself through what others say, see, or think about you, but allow God to tell you who you are in Him. He has a new name for you, one that will encapsulate all that you are. Even if everything was strong at the beginning, God can change your life if you allow Him to tell you who you are in His eyes. Jephthah was not an outcast in God's sight; he was a mighty man of valor.

From a cultural point of view, the turning away of the children of Israel from God happened the year the last judge, Jair, died. It did not take long for them to drift away from God. Judges were established to free the children of Israel in times of oppression and should rule over them under God's direction. However, the children of Israel followed Jair more than they followed God and His Law. Reading through the Judges, the story repeats itself: The Israelites did well when they had a leader. They did not, once that leader had passed. They needed a constant human reminder because the Law was not engraved on their hearts. They did not meditate on it; they did not keep the Lord at heart. They were followers of men more than they were followers of God. Follow God; don't follow men.

On a spiritual point of view, when you abandon the Lord of Heaven to follow other gods like the children of Israel did, you open your house and your heart to everything and anything: every trend, every wind, every idea. Nothing will satisfy you, and you will become vulnerable to every passing breeze, like the Israelites who adopted every god possible after the death of Jair. Print God's Law on your heart; let it shape your attitude and expectations. The Law and the fear of the Lord will be your constant reminders and the standards by which you live each day. How do you do this? Through continuous study of God's Word, engaging in daily reading. To quote Joshua 1:8, "This Book of the Law shall not depart from your mouth, but you shall meditate in it day and night, that you may observe to do according to all that is written in it. For then you will make your way prosperous, and then you will have success." If you switch allegiance and abandon God like the Israelites did, your life will become a constant struggle because you will know the truth, but because you rejected it, it will not set you free. Abandoning God means choosing Satan. There is no middle ground—no gray area in this fight. It's either one or the other. When Paul said, "wretched man that I am!" (Romans 7:24–25), he was not describing his present state because he had been freed when he met Jesus. He was telling of a person who knows the Law and the solution to sin but still allows sin to dwell in his heart and does not make a clear decision, compromising instead of making a precise cut. God asks for a definitive choice. Light and darkness cannot coexist. You must choose whom to follow. You cannot obey God and sin daily. The Bible is clear. In Judges 10:6, the children of Israel experienced great suffering because of their compromise and abandonment of God.

When you find yourself in periods of inactivity, overwise known as desert, it could mean several things: a necessary time for rest or training. A desert isn't always a negative place to be, even if it certainly feels like it. So, when you are in a desert time, work for the Lord. Use this time to read, study, train, and rest. Life is an alternation of seasons, and just as God rested on the seventh day of Creation Week, we, too, experience times of rest and growth. Remember that you are only a pilgrim on this planet, and your opportunity to make a difference is not only brief but also passes quickly. When accepting a mission from God, responding to a call, or engaging in any work—whether secular or religious— never forget to include God in your decisions. In fact, make sure to include Him in every part of your life.

Finally, like Jephthah, do not avoid your problems. Once they come to light, confront them directly, address the issue, and find its root causes. Whether it's sin, neglect, evil, or an old covenant, bring it into the light and the truth of the Gospel. Confront the problem and restore the truth, because truth will set you free.

Jephthah's beginnings were not very good. However, the Lord is greater than our ancestors' faults, greater than our sins, and He is gracious enough to forgive us if we come to Him with a repentant heart. He sees us differently from how the world sees us. When walking with God, the end is more important than the beginning. Life is not a sprint; it's a marathon, and as we move forward, opportunities arise to reverse curses and turn them into blessings. You can change direction and transform circumstances. Be filled with the Spirit every day. May He be your constant companion and guide in your decisions and leadership.

The beauty of walking with the Lord is that we can move forward confidently because we are never alone.

WALK BY FAITH EVERY DAY

"Not that I have already attained, or am already perfected; but I press on, that I may lay hold of that for which Christ Jesus has also laid hold of me. Brethren, I do not count myself to have apprehended; but one thing I do, forgetting those things which are behind and reaching forward to those things which are ahead, I press toward the goal for the prize of the upward call of God in Christ Jesus" (Philippians 2: 12–14).

REFLECTION QUESTIONS

Take a minute to think about how you perceive yourself. Do you suffer from low self-esteem? Are you basing the definition of your identity on what other people say, or do you rely on the Lord? Which one is (or should be) the most important? What can you do to change this today?

JAEL AND HEBER

At times, we find ourselves engrossed in the routine of life, when, out of the blue, an opportunity to make a significant difference presents itself. How will we respond to these unexpected moments? In such instances, the stories of Jael and Heber the Kenite can serve as guiding lights, inspiring us to act with courage and faith at the right time.

Jael, a woman living a simple life in her tent, was unexpectedly given the opportunity to make a profound difference. She was married to Heber the Kenite, a man of ordinary standing. Judges 4:11 states that Heber was among the descendants of Hobab, Moses' father-in-law, and a member of the Kenite people. The Kenites were longtime allies of the Israelites. The father-in-law of Moses was a Kenite; he was known for giving Moses advice on how to judge the affairs of the Hebrews. Also, when Israel emerged from the desert after the second forty-year journey and prepared to conquer the Promised Land, the Kenites walked alongside the Israelites between the City of Palms and the desert of Judah (Judges 1:16). They consistently showed kindness to the children of Israel. However, Judges 4:17 states that the Kenites lived in peace with King Jabin, who was the enemy of the Israelites. Therefore, Jael and Heber were in no way concerned by the war between Jabin and the Israelites. However, in the days of Heber and Jael, the Kenites had decided to switch allegiance: They turned their backs on the Israelites when they betrayed them and warned Jabin of Barak's strategic move to Mount Tabor in Judges 4:12.

Given his reaction, it seems that Heber disagreed with this new alliance, which betrayed their longtime friends, and he severed ties with his people, moving his tents near the terebinth tree at Zaanaim, which is beside Kedesh. As a result, when the enemy of the Israelites, the general of Jabin's army, himself entered their tent, Jael did not think twice and fought for her friends, freeing them from oppression and handing them the victory. She killed Sisera, the general of King Jabin's army.

The service and availability of Jael and Heber are examples to follow and learn from.

First, as Heber did, sever all ties with sin and idolatry. King Jabin was a Canaanite, a people whose religion was abhorrent to the Lord and who fought against Israel for a long time. Heber separated himself from the other members of his tribe who had decided to be at peace with Jabin; however, Jabin was at war with Israel. Keeping ties with past sins and sometimes past relationships can hinder your walk with God and create stumbling blocks on your journey.

Second, like Heber, choose your allies wisely. Heber and Jael were allies of Israel; however, the other members of their group were no longer so. Old friends can betray, new friends can save, and the reverse can also be true. Use discernment when selecting your friends and surround yourself with people who are like-minded, encouraging, believers, and faith-builders. Remember the advice from King Solomon and Apostle Paul: "Whoever walks with the wise becomes wise, but the companion of fools will suffer harm" (Proverbs 13:20) and "Bad company corrupts good morals" (1 Corinthians 15:33). The habits and behaviors of the people around you will influence you. Their attitude will also impact your decision-making and daily life. True friends will work to set you free, just as Jael was instrumental in freeing the Israelites from the yoke of the Canaanites. Bad friends will hinder you.

Show kindness to those around you. It will be a blessing for you and your descendants. If people remember a wrong done, they also remember a right or an act of kindness and share it with others. A little kindness can go a long way, especially spiritually. The Lord never forgot the kindness of the Kenites toward the children of Israel, and their kindness was rewarded multiple times in the following generations. The Israelites always remembered them and spared them during wars, and sometimes rewarded them. King Saul warned the Kenites of the coming war against the Amalekites in 1 Samuel 15:6. King David shared in the spoil taken from the Amalekites in 1 Samuel 30:29.

Sometimes, we are busy with life when suddenly the Lord needs us. As situations arise, how will we react? The answer is simple: Take God's side (to quote the leader of the Bible study group where I go) and do the right thing!

WALK BY FAITH EVERY DAY

"Fear not, for I am with you;
Be not dismayed, for I am your God.
I will strengthen you,
Yes, I will help you,
I will uphold you with My righteous right hand"
(Isaiah 41:10).

REFLECTION QUESTIONS

Do you find yourself busy with life to the point of neglecting your prayer life or Bible study time? What can you do today to remediate this issue? How do you think correcting this trajectory will help you in your everyday life, your work life, and your spiritual life?

PART 12

Those Who Chose Truth

Illustration 12: Nicodemus

Absolute truth figures now on the list of endangered ideas. Our world is inundated with relativistic philosophies and the superiority of personal experience at an alarming rate, thanks to Post-Modernism. However, truth speaks and is born from facts: Science can say all it wants, but the world was created in one way, and one way only—the way it actually happened. Men and women in the Bible chose the truth over the lies of their time and, as a consequence, either endured persecution and mockery from their fellow relativist humanist human beings or were changed forever.

Micaiah and Nicodemus were two of the men who chose the truth, held on to it, and were transformed.

MICAIAH

Sometimes, when we speak the truth, we get slapped in the face. And sometimes, when we talk about the truth, we get jailed. Both happened to Micaiah because he chose to tell the truth to his king, despite the orders he had been given. Still, we should continue fighting for the truth because it is the only thing that will set those around us free.

The name Micaiah means "Who is like the Lord?" in Hebrew. He was the son of Imlah. Although he was from the tribe of Judah (located to the south), he lived in the kingdom of Israel, near Samaria. Micaiah served as a prophet of the Lord in Israel in troubled times, around the same time as Elijah. The evil King Ahab and his wife, Jezebel, were then the rulers of the Northern Kingdom of Israel. Micaiah served the Lord, proclaiming, "Who is like the Lord?" amid an idolatrous people devoted to the worship of Baal. We know he had visions of the Lord and revelations of Heaven's courts. He even saw what was happening before the Throne of the Lord. During his life and ministry, idolatrous Ahab and Jezebel reigned over Israel from Samaria, and Jehoshaphat, a follower of the Lord, was king of Judah. The arrival of Micaiah at the court of the king of Israel was a result of the clash between these two worldviews. It concerned the decision for Israel to go to war against the king of Aram to retrieve Ramoth in Gilead or not. No other kings worked together who were more apart in terms of ethics and spirituality than these two kings. On one throne was Ahab, the son of Omri. He ruled Israel, the Northern Kingdom, for twenty-two years from Samaria. He was married to Jezebel, an evil Sidonian princess. He did evil in the eyes of the Lord and adopted his wife's paganistic way of life, worshipping the Baals.

Micaiah served as a referee between truth and lies, proclaiming the supremacy of the Lord over every other power on set. He acted as a referee between two opposing worldviews, pointing out the truth and exposing the lies. The things he prophesied were publicly displayed. There was no doubt about the integrity of his ministry: Even Ahab knew him and presented him in those terms "There is still one prophet through whom we can inquire of the Lord, but I hate him because he never prophesies anything good about me, but always bad. He is Micaiah son of Imlah" (1 Kings 22:8).

At the time of the events narrated in 2 Kings 22, there had been peace between Syria and Israel for three years after Ahab repented and humiliated himself before the Lord following

Elijah's words (1 Kings 21:21–24). He even wore the sack and the ashes in his house (1 Kings 21:27). However, Ahab still had Satan in his home through Jezebel. And although everything was going well, he was going to engage in a war with Syria because he did not shut the door to Satan. On the other side was Jehoshaphat. Jehoshaphat was the son of Asa, who reigned over the Southern Kingdom of Judah from Jerusalem. Jehoshaphat was thirty-five when he became king and reigned for twenty-five years in Jerusalem. His mother was Azuba. Jehoshaphat walked in David's steps, and the Lord was with him (2 Chronicles 17:1–4). Peace and prosperity defined his reign, and the fear of the Lord took over all the people surrounding Judah (2 Chronicles 17:10). However, he established a covenant through marriage with the house of Ahab: Jehoshaphat's son, Jehoram, married one of the daughters of Ahab, Athaliah, which led Jehoram to choose evil once in power. As long as Satan has a foot in the house (a Jezebel or an Athaliah), he will not leave anyone dwelling in this house alone. Things might go well for a while, but it won't last.

After listening to the false prophet standing in King Ahab's court regarding the decision to go to war, King Jehoshaphat intervened. He was a truth-seeker and a king devoted to the Lord, so discernment set in. He knew all these prophets, then standing before him and Ahab, were false. What is extraordinary in this story is that Ahab also knew all the prophets standing before him were false prophets, and that the only true prophets were absent. He consciously invited people he knew would tell him what he wanted to hear. Everyone knew Micaiah as a true prophet of the Lord. From King Ahab, who consciously did not invite him to the prophetic gathering, to the messengers sent to get him who were trying to influence his words because they knew his words would contradict everyone else: "Then the messenger who had gone to call Micaiah spoke to him, saying, 'Now listen, the words of the prophets with one accord encourage the king. Please, let your word be like the word of one of them and speak encouragement'" (1 Kings 22:13). They knew the prophets were telling their king lies and were okay with it.

Micaiah's example is an inspiration to stand for the truth. Here is how: In 1 Kings 22:8, Ahab says he hates Micaiah when Jehoshaphat asks to listen to him because he never said good things about him. Ahab liked to hear the things that tickled his ears, getting what he wanted and never encountering contradiction. Jezabel had mastered the art of flattery and ear tickling. (see the episode of Naboth's vineyard in 1 Kings 21). However, this ultimately led to his death on the battlefield, as recorded in 2 Kings 22. The world hates the truth and the truth-tellers who proclaim it, and its lies will take people to their deaths. Satan will give you what you want to keep you hooked, just as Jezebel did with Ahab. However, tell the truth; shine the light. If the ones around you listen, they could be saved and their lives transformed.

Ahab continued to reject the truth. He hated it and its bearer (his words!). The fact is that after rejecting the truth for some time, the Lord will send us what we want to hear, because we will seek out those things and surround ourselves with people who tell us what we want to hear, not what the Lord has to say (see also Balaam's story in Numbers 22–24). There had been a threshold that had been crossed by Ahab, a point of no return to which truth became intolerable.

Many prophets were invited except Micaiah, who was excluded. Choosing truth will not get us invited to gatherings and other parties because, like Micaiah, who constantly reminds those surrounding him that the Lord was unique, the presence of the disciples of Jesus Christ, filled with the Holy Spirit, disturbs evil. It shines a light on people's consciences and hearts. It's a constant reminder that there is something wrong with those who choose to follow Satan. Remember that not to follow Christ means to follow Satan; there is no third option.

Lastly, just as Ahab knew that Micaiah would come against everything said by the other prophets, if you choose the truth, people will know you for what you stand for and may even try to smother your words before you begin speaking.

In conclusion, some soldiers fight with natural weapons, others with the words Jesus said: "The truth will set you free" (John 8:32). Like Micaiah, choose and tell the truth because lies always cause trouble. In this case, lies lead to Ahab's death. Wear truth like a belt (Ephesians 6:14); it is part of the soldier's equipment because it holds everything together. Accept to stand aside and be more concerned about what the Lord thinks of you than what the world thinks. Micaiah stood before the king and did his job. We don't hear about him after. Was he released from prison? We don't know. One thing is sure: The people realized he was hearing from the Lord because Ahab died on the battlefield.

WALK BY FAITH EVERY DAY

"Then Jesus said to those Jews who believed Him, 'If you abide in My word, you are My disciples indeed. And you shall know the truth, and the truth shall make you free'" (John 8:31–32).

REFLECTION QUESTIONS

Consider Micaiah's words in the presence of King Ahab and Jehoshaphat. How did the two kings perceive the prophet? Why? How did Micaiah serve as a referee between these two worldviews?

Following this discussion, Ahab engaged in a war against the king of Aram and was killed in battle. In what way was Micaiah a true prophet of the Lord?

NICODEMUS

Religious traditions and old lies are among the most challenging ideas to drive out. They shape us, they define us, and they build our reputation. They represent man's foolish foundations that will fail when the tempest comes and leads to destruction. Only truth can shake these old walls and rebuild solid, divine foundations. This is what happened to Nicodemus.

Nicodemus was an old, respectable man, likely a wealthy one, who wielded influence in the religious, judicial, and political spheres. As a member of the Pharisee sect, he had spent his life learning the Torah and working to apply and respect the Law all his life. As for all Pharisees, his goal was to be a role model for the Jews to follow to attain a priest-like spiritual purity in their daily life. As a member of the Sanhedrin, he was a leader of the Jewish people, a legislator, and a judge. In summary, everybody knew Nicodemus, or at least was familiar with him, and as such, he was respected. He was a public figure with a public image to maintain and a reputation to uphold. However, his foundations were shaken by the coming and the teachings of Jesus Christ. Even though he was a Pharisee, he did not follow the consensus, which was to reject Jesus Christ as the Messiah and to deny the truth. Like a moth, he found himself attracted to the light of the truth. By night, he came to Jesus, risking consequences from his fellow Pharisees who hated Jesus Christ and sought to have him killed. Because of his decision, he received the revelation of the truth. In his opening statement, when first meeting Jesus in John 3, Nicodemus did not say that he knew Jesus had come from God. He did not say "I know" but used the personal pronoun "we," which points to either the group of the Pharisees in general, or the Sanhedrin: "Rabbi, we know that You are a teacher come from God; for no one can do these signs that You do unless God is with him" (John 3:2). The people surrounding him knew the true identity of Jesus Christ, still they chose to smother it and silence it. He decided to go and inquire for himself.

When Nicodemus came to see Jesus, he did not appear boastful or proud. He came to ask questions, in humility, ready to hear what Jesus had to say. Talking to Jesus, he said "Rabbi," which means teacher, admitting Jesus' superior knowledge of God and the Law (which is a lot for a Pharisee!)

Even though he came by night, he came! He was a silent voice among Pharisees who saw the truth, and contrary to them, he recognized it. Perhaps it was not a sudden realization. Perhaps, it came gradually. However, once he faced the truth, he was no longer the same. The words of Jesus initiated a transformation that is narrated in the Gospel of John. Although we do not know what happened after this conversation, we know that Nicodemus, who first hid in the shadow of the night, took a stand in front of all the Pharisees in John 7:50. In John 7, following Jesus' teachings at the Feast of Tabernacles, the crowd became very divided, many rooting for him, others insulting him. The Pharisees even sent soldiers to silence Jesus. However, the Pharisees were left dumbfounded and probably humiliated by the soldiers' positive response to Jesus. Just as Nicodemus, the soldiers were transformed, or at least shaken in their beliefs, by the hearing of Jesus Christ's words. The Pharisees grew very angry and fussed at the men: "Are you also deceived? Have any of the rulers or the Pharisees believed in Him? But this crowd that does not know the law is accursed" (John 7:46). It is at that moment that Nicodemus stood out of the shadows and prove them wrong in their generalizing assumption that rulers and Pharisees did not believe in him, dissolving the crowd that was angry against Jesus. Although he did not openly claim to be a follower of Jesus Christ, his taking a stand against the crowd and other members of the Sanhedrin or the Pharisees group demonstrates a change in his heart and his perception of Jesus Christ: "Nicodemus (he who came to Jesus by night, being one of them) said to them, "Does our law judge a man before it hears him and knows what he is doing?" (John 7:50–51).

The change reached full accomplishment in John 19. Many today remember that Joseph of Arimathea requested the body of Jesus to give him a proper burial. However, many forget, or ignore, that Nicodemus was with him to take the body from the cross (John 19:38–41), and that he brought "a mixture of myrrh and aloes, about a hundred pounds weight" (John 19:39). A hundred pounds of spices and herbs is a lot to carry, so he probably had servants with him. As such, he became a witness to his new faith, choosing truth over tradition and the rule of God, in front of his household, the other Pharisees, and the Sanhedrin. He had to really love Jesus Christ to invest so much of his wealth in the embalmment. Historians agree that he brought twice what was necessary for a standard burial, and some estimate the value of the load to stand between $150,000 and $200,000 in today's money. Such a gift for a person who has died testifies to the high esteem Nicodemus held Jesus in and that he wanted to give Jesus the burial of a king out of respect and honor. His heart was changed.

So, how does Nicodemus inspire us today, and what can we learn from him?

The groups to which we belong become part of our identity. However, that does not mean we should follow them mindlessly. Like Nicodemus, begin by analyzing the facts and the signs for yourself. When the truth comes to you, do not silence it but ask the questions. Jesus promised that those who ask will receive. Regardless of your position in society, you have a role and a mission to fulfill. The Bible tells you why you are on this planet. Let the truth of the Gospel guide you like a light in darkness, and answer your most personal, challenging questions.

As Nicodemus came into the night to meet Jesus, until you face the truth and acknowledge it, you move and live in the darkness. The truth is what will set you free and work its transformation in you. Ultimately, Nicodemus came to accept the divine origin of Jesus. He was shaken by everything he witnessed: the miracles, the healings, the teachings. If Nicodemus discussed all these signs when he first met Jesus, it means the Pharisees and the Sanhedrin also discussed Jesus and were deeply disturbed by everything that was happening. For the Pharisees, the only way to recognize the divine origin was to compare Jesus with men of the Old Testament: They had Moses, Elijah, and Elisha, and many others, but everything pointed to a divine origin of Jesus Christ, not a human one. Because Nicodemus was honest in his approach, he received the revelation of salvation and what it means to be born again. He also received the revelation that Jesus Christ was the Son of God, since it's in Jesus' response to Nicodemus that we find the famous John 3:16 verse.

Like Nicodemus, leave the truth to transform you, set you free, and shine the light of Jesus Christ through your actions in front of your household and the workplace. Actual change on the inside is visible on the outside. Worship Jesus as the King He is; bring your offering to Him generously.

We don't hear about Nicodemus after the burial; however, his actions continue to be discussed today. God honored the faith and faithfulness of that man who chose truth over lies by having him remembered and his actions placed in the Gospel of John to teach us today to take a stand and be generous until the end.

WALK BY FAITH EVERY DAY

"For God so loved the world that He gave His only begotten Son, that whoever believes in Him should not perish but have everlasting life" (John 3:16).

REFLECTION QUESTIONS

Consider Nicodemus' evolution in the faith and his knowledge of Jesus Christ, as well as the steps he took. How did he stand out from the groups he belonged to? How did he change those around him? How can you take a stand like him and influence your household, your workplace, and your family for God?

A THANK YOU NOTE AND SOME FINAL THOUGHTS

Thank you for picking up this copy of *(Extra)Ordinary*. We hope that the stories and life testimonies of these 35 men and women have inspired you to trust the Lord and take a stand for His glory, build His Kingdom and leave a spiritual legacy that will transform your family tree, break the curses and bless those coming after you. What transpires from these pages is that we are all part of a Kingdom and engaged in a spiritual army that is as diverse as its individuals. Your impact, even though small actions and decisions, can change the lives of your people, change your community and the alter the world. As I wrote already in the previous pages, we are not all called to stand on a stage, but we are all called to serve. So, make a decision today to choose God's side in your life, in the work place, in your family. The repercussions will resound both in the natural and the spiritual realms and you will leave a lasting transforming blessing legacy!

GENERAL DISCUSSION QUESTIONS

Below is a series of questions to make you consider everything you learn in this book. These questions can be answered individually or in a group setting, such as a Bible study group.

1. To which character did you relate the most? Why?
2. How did he or she encourage you?
3. What will you do today, tomorrow, to be more like that character?
4. Which one of these traits do you think is your strong suit? And why?
   - Faith
   - Wisdom
   - Perseverance
   - Generosity
   - Courage
   - Truth seeker

- Faithfulness
- Trustworthy
- Loyalty
- Humility

5. Which one do you think you need the most now? What can you do to increase your knowledge and experience of it?

A CHRONOLOGY OF THE CHARACTERS MENTIONED IN (EXTRA)ORDINARY

ca. 3382–3017 BC: Enoch

ca. 2100–1800 BC: Abraham's servant

ca. 1930–1840 BC: Hagar

ca. 15–13th century BC:

- Shiphrah and Puah
- Yokebed
- Miriam
- Bezalel
- Oholiab
- Caleb
- Rahab

ca. 12th century BC:

- Deborah
- Jael

- Joash
- Jephthah

ca. 11th century BC:

- Hannah
- Asaph
- Obed-Edom

ca. 10th century BC:

- Abigail
- The people of Jabesh-Gilead
- Shobi, Machir, and Barzillai
- A woman of Abel of Beth-Maachah
- The thirty-seven mighty men of King David

9th century BC:

- The widow of Zarephath
- Micaiah

1st century AD:

- The shepherds
- The magi
- Zacchaeus
- The Samaritan woman
- Joanna, Susanna, Mary-Magdalene
- The four men of relentless faith
- Joseph of Arimathea
- Nicodemus
- Ananias
- Luke

APPENDIX C

LIST OF READINGS

- HAGAR Genesis 16:1–16 and Genesis 21:8–1

- HANNAH 1 Samuel 1 and 2

- ZACCHAEUS Luke 19:1–10

- OBED-EDOM 2 Samuel 6:10–12

- BARZILLAI 2 Samuel 19:31–39

- THE PEOPLE OF JABESH-GILEAD 1 Samuel 31:8–13 and 2 Samuel 2:4–7

- ENOCH Genesis 5:21–24 and Jude v.14

- THE WIDOW OF ZAREPHATH 1 Kings 17

- THE SHEPHERDS Luke 2:8–19

- THE SAMARITAN WOMAN John 4

- RAHAB Joshua 2, and 6:22–25

- JOASH Judges 6

- SHOBI, MACHIR, AND BARZILLAI 2 Samuel 17:27, 2 Samuel 19:31–39, 1 Kings 2:7

- BEZALEL Exodus 31

- OHOLIAB Exodus 38:23

- ASAPH Psalms 50, 73–83

- THE MAGI Matthew 2:1–23

- JOANNA, SUSANNA, MARY MAGDALENE, AND MANY OTHERS Luke 8:2, **3**

- CALEB Numbers 13 and 14

- THE THIRTY-SEVEN MIGHTY MEN OF KING DAVID 2 Samuel 23:8–39

- THE FOUR MEN OF RELENTLESS FAITH Mark 2:3–5 and Luke 5:18–25

- ABRAHAM'S SERVANT Genesis 24

- DEBORAH Judges 4 and 5

- ABIGAIL, WIFE OF NABAL 1 Samuel 25

- A WOMAN OF ABEL OF BETH MAACHAH 2 Samuel 20: 16–22

- LUKE Gospel According to Luke and book of Acts, Colossians 4:14, Philemon v.24, 2 Timothy 4:11

- JOSEPH OF ARIMATHEA Matthew 27:57–60; Mark 15:42–47; Luke 23:50–56; and John 18:38–42

- ANANIAS Acts 9:10–19

- SHIPHRAH AND PUAH Exodus 1:15–21

- YOKEBED Exodus 2:1–3

- MIRIAM Exodus 2:4 and 7

- JEPHTHAH Judges 10:6, 11–33

- JAEL AND HEBER Judges 4:17–23

- MICAIAH 1 Kings 22

- NICODEMUS John 3, John 7, and John 19

ACKNOWLEDGMENTS

Thank You, Lord, for entrusting me with this message. I hope I was up to the task and that it will bring hope to those who read it. It is now in Your hand.

Thank you to my husband for his unwavering faith in me and for whatever I put my mind to. I have come to his office so many times with so many new ideas and projects. You never talked me out of doing it. I know it can be difficult to follow me sometimes, still your encouragements and faith were the fuel that kept me going.

WE WOULD LOVE TO HEAR FROM YOU!

Dear Reader,

Thank you so much for reading my book. It means the world to me. If you found it helpful, inspiring, or enjoyable, please leave a review. Your feedback not only helps others decide whether they will read it or not, but also keeps me motivated to create more valuable content for you.

Your kind words make a difference. Thank you for your support.

ABOUT THE AUTHOR

Born in the Parisian suburbs, M.D. Crackower grew up hearing the testimonies and miracles of her parents, grandparents, and great-grandparents. Later on, her academic journey took her to Greece, where she studied ancient Greek History and in the mission field in Niger and Morocco. Today, M.D. Crackower works as a Senior Instructor at a southern university. She holds a PhD in Francophone Studies and studies 19th-century French literature and language pedagogy. However, apologetics and the study of the Bible remain her favorite topics.

M. D. Crackower is an educator and author dedicated to making the Bible both understandable and deeply meaningful for modern readers. With a background in education and a passion for biblical scholarship, she explores Scripture through historical context, narrative insight, and practical reflection. Her writing bridges academic depth and spiritual encouragement, helping readers connect timeless biblical truths to everyday life and personal faith journeys.

OTHER BOOKS BY M.D. CRACKOWER

(Published and forthcoming)

Strategy: A Divine Blueprint for Spiritual Battles. Wise Owls Publishing house, 2025

This Bible commentary on the book of Nehemiah aims to research and analyze the strategic behavior that animated Nehemiah, eventually driving him to succeed in his endeavor for the LORD. It also explains how, today, we can do the same and win in spiritual battles.

FORTHCOMING BOOKS IN THE *BIBLICAL PERSPECTIVES SERIES* BY M.D. CRACKOWER!

BIBLICAL PERSPECTIVES SERIES

Biblical Perspectives is a series of standalone books that explore some of the most significant themes of the Bible, such as (but not limited to):

- *The Divinity of Christ* (forthcoming in 2026)
- *Wisdom* (forthcoming in 2026)

- *Joy* (forthcoming in 2027)
- *Peace* (forthcoming in 2027)

Each book in this new series is written following the same principles, where the Bible is used to explain the Bible, and scholarly and historical research delves into the complexities of the context to bring the texts to life. This works together to make these books as informative as possible. Combined with life application, the Biblical Perspectives series aims to draw readers closer to God and foster a more profound love and understanding of the Word of God.

The idea behind this series is to increase the reader's faith and understanding of the Word of God, while providing them with the tools to explain biblical texts and defend the faith more effectively.